7 Streams of Wealth

Eric Ramsey

Copyrighted Material

Copyright ©2024 by Eric Ramsey

All rights reserved.

No part of this book may be reproduced, stored in a retrieval system, or transmitted in any form or by any means electronic, mechanical, photocopying, recording, or otherwise without prior written permission from the copyright holder, except for brief quotations in critical reviews and certain other noncommercial uses permitted by copyright law.

ISBN: 9798335994965

Imprint: Independently published

Dedication

To my family, whose unwavering support and encouragement have been the bedrock of my journey. And to every reader seeking to build a prosperous and secure future – may this book serve as a beacon on your path to wealth and fulfillment.

Table Of Contents

Introduction..9

Chapter 1
Capital Gains..15
Introduction to Capital Gains… (15)
Types of Capital Gains… (17)
Strategies for Maximizing Capital Gains… (20)
Tax Implications and Planning… (23)
Case Studies… (26)
Mitigation Strategies… (31)

Chapter 2
Interest Income..39
Introduction to Interest Income… (39)
Types of Interest Income… (41)
Maximizing Interest Income… (44)
Tax Implications and Strategies for Interest Income… (47)
Case Studies… (50)
Risks and Mitigation Strategies… (51)

Chapter 3
Earned Income..54
1. Introduction to Earned Income… (54)
2. Traditional Employment… (54)
    - Benefits and Drawbacks of Traditional Employment… (55)
    - Salary Negotiation and Job Market Trends… (56)
    - Job Market Trends… (57)
3. Freelancing and Gig Economy… (58)
    - Pros and Cons… (59)
    - Platforms and Opportunities… (61)
4. Entrepreneurship and Small Businesses… (62)
    - Starting Your Own Business… (62)
    - Challenges and Rewards… (63)

5. Consulting and Professional Services... (65)
   - Types of Consulting Work... (66)
   - Building a Consulting Business
   - Success Stories... (67)
6. Side Hustles... (67)
   - Balancing with a Full-time Job... (68)
   - Case Studies... (68)
7. Increasing Your Earned Income... (69)
   - Career Advancement... (69)
   - Continuing Education and Skill Development... (70)
   - Networking and Personal Branding... (70)
8. Managing and Optimizing Earned Income... (71)
   - Budgeting and Saving... (71)
   - Investing Wisely... (72)
   - Tax Considerations... (73)

Chapter 4

Resale Profit..75
1. Introduction to Resale Profit... (75)
2. Types of Resale Businesses... (75)
   - Step-By-Step Guide To Retail Arbitrage... (76)
   - Online Marketplaces... (79)
   - Detailed Guide to Online Marketplaces... (80)
   - Key Investments for Successful Sellers... (82)
   - Real Estate Flipping... (83)
   - Strategies for Successful Real Estate Flipping... (83)
   - Collectibles and Antiques... (86)
   - Essential Strategies for Reselling Collectibles and Antiques.. (87)
   - Brick-and-Mortar Resale Shops... (89)
   - Types and Benefits of Brick-and-Mortar Resale Shops... (89)
   - Flea Markets and Garage Sales... (92)
   - Consignment Shops... (94)
   - How Consignment Shops Work... (94)
   - Advantages of Consignment Shops... (95)

3. Finding Resale Opportunities... (97)
- Market Research... (97)
- Sourcing Products... (98)
- Evaluating Potential Profitability... (99)

4. Valuing and Pricing Items... (100)
- Assessing Item Value... (101)
- Pricing Strategies... (101)
- Market Considerations... (104)

5. Selling Platforms and Strategies... (105)
- Online Platforms... (105)
- Social Media and Personal Websites... (107)
- Offline Selling Strategies... (108)

6. Strategies for Maximizing Resale Profit... (108)
- Building a Brand... (109)
- Effective Marketing Techniques... (109)
- Customer Engagement and Retention... (110)
- Pricing Strategies... (111)
- Negotiation Techniques... (111)

7. Operational Considerations... (112)
- Inventory Management... (112)
- Shipping and Logistics... (113)
- Financial Tracking and Reporting... (114)

8. Case Studies... (115)
9. Challenges and Solutions... (117)

Chapter 5

Rental Property..122

1. Introduction to Rental Property... (122)
2. Types of Rental Properties... (124)
3. Steps to Investing in Rental Properties... (129)
4. Managing Rental Properties... (135)
5. Maximizing Rental Income... (140)
6. Case Studies... (146)
7. Tax Implications and Legal Considerations... (149)

Chapter 6

Dividend Income...156
1. Definition and Overview... (156)
2. Benefits and Drawbacks: Weighing the Pros and Cons... (158)
3. Identifying Dividend-Paying Investments... (160)
   - Factors to Consider When Choosing Dividend-Paying Stocks... (160)
   - Examples of Dividend-Paying Stocks... (161)
   - Mutual Funds and ETFs: Diversified Dividend Income.. (162)
   - Benefits of Mutual Funds and ETFs... (162)
   - Examples of Dividend-Focused Mutual Funds and ETFs...(163)
4. Real Estate Investment Trusts (REITs)... (164)
   - How REITs Work... (164)
   - Benefits and Risks for Investors... (165)
5. Strategies for Maximizing Dividend Income... (166)
6. Evaluating Company Health and Sustainability... (172)
   - Key Financial Ratios for Dividend Investors... (172)
7. Case Studies... (176)
8. A Step-by-Step Guide to Starting Dividend Investing... (177)

Chapter 7

Royalties..184
1. Introduction to Royalties... (184)
2. Types of Royalties: An Exploration... (186)
3. How Royalties Work... (188)
4. Generating Royalties from Intellectual Property... (191)
5. Legal Aspects of Royalties... (197)
6. Strategies to Maximize Royalty Income... (200)
7. Challenges and Risks... (204)
8. Future Trends in Royalties... (207)

Introduction

In a rapidly evolving economic landscape, the pursuit of financial stability and growth has never been more critical. The concept of building wealth transcends the mere accumulation of money; it embodies the creation of financial security, freedom, and the ability to lead a fulfilling life without monetary constraints. "7 Streams of Wealth" is crafted to serve as a comprehensive guide for individuals seeking to navigate the multifaceted world of wealth creation. By breaking down the complex terrain of income generation into seven fundamental streams, this book aims to provide readers with actionable insights and practical strategies to achieve and sustain financial prosperity.

Understanding Wealth

Wealth is often misunderstood as a singular, static concept. In reality, it is dynamic and multifaceted, encompassing various forms of income and assets that contribute to an individual's financial well-being. The journey to wealth involves not only earning money but also making informed decisions about saving, investing, and managing assets. This book's primary objective is to shed light on the diverse avenues through which wealth can be built, maintained, and grown over time.

The Importance of Multiple Income Streams

Relying on a single source of income can be precarious, as it exposes individuals to the risk of financial instability in the event of job loss, economic downturns, or unexpected expenses. Diversifying income streams is a proven strategy to mitigate risk and enhance financial security. By establishing multiple sources of income, individuals can create a more resilient financial foundation, ensuring that they are better equipped to weather economic fluctuations and capitalize on opportunities for growth.

The Seven Streams of Wealth

The seven streams of wealth explored in this book are:

Capital Gains
Interest Income
Earned Income
Resale Profit
Rental Property
Dividend Income
Royalties

Each of these streams offers unique advantages and opportunities for income generation. By understanding and strategically leveraging these streams, individuals can create a diversified and robust portfolio of income sources.

Capital Gains

Capital gains are profits realized from the sale of assets that have appreciated in value. This stream encompasses a wide range of investments, including stocks, real estate, and collectibles. Capital gains can provide significant returns, but they also require a deep understanding of market dynamics, investment strategies, and tax implications. This book delves into the intricacies of capital gains, offering insights into maximizing returns through strategic asset selection and timing.

Interest Income

Interest income is earned from lending money or investing in interest-bearing accounts and instruments. This stream includes traditional savings accounts, certificates of deposit (CDs), bonds, and peer-to-peer lending platforms. Interest income offers a relatively stable and predictable source of revenue, making it an essential component of a diversified income strategy. The book explores various ways to maximize interest income by understanding the interest rate environment, diversifying investments, and reinvesting earnings.

Earned Income

Earned income is the money obtained from active work, whether as an employee or through self-employment. It is the most familiar and straightforward form of income but also the most taxing in terms of time and effort. This chapter provides strategies for enhancing earned income through career advancement, entrepreneurship, and supplementary side hustles. By focusing on skill development and strategic career moves, individuals can significantly increase their earning potential.

Resale Profit

Resale profit is generated from buying items at a lower price and selling them at a higher price. This stream involves retail arbitrage, flipping products, and trading in antiques and collectibles. Resale profit can be a lucrative income stream with the right market research, negotiation skills, and understanding of online marketplaces. The book provides detailed strategies for identifying profitable resale opportunities and maximizing margins.

Rental Property

Rental income is earned from leasing property to tenants. This stream includes residential, commercial, and vacation rental properties. Rental property can provide a steady stream of passive income, but it requires careful property selection, tenant management, and financing strategies. The book offers insights into building a successful rental property portfolio, from choosing high-demand areas to maintaining properties and managing tenants effectively.

Dividend Income

Dividend income is earned from owning shares in companies that distribute a portion of their profits to shareholders. This stream focuses on building a dividend portfolio by selecting reliable, high-yield dividend stocks, utilizing dividend reinvestment plans (DRIPs), and diversifying investments across different sectors. Dividend income can be a powerful tool for wealth accumulation, providing regular payouts and the potential for compounding returns over time.

Royalties

Royalties are payments received for the use of intellectual property, such as books, music, patents, and trademarks. This stream encompasses earnings from publishing, songwriting, licensing patents, and other creative endeavors. Royalties can provide a continuous and passive income stream, but they require creating valuable intellectual property and negotiating favorable licensing agreements. The book explores strategies for maximizing royalty income through effective marketing, promotion, and intellectual property management.

"7 Streams of Wealth" is designed to empower readers with the knowledge and tools necessary to diversify their income sources and achieve financial independence. Each chapter offers a deep dive into one of the seven streams, providing practical advice, real-life examples, and actionable strategies. By embracing the principles outlined in this book, readers can take control of their financial future, reduce their reliance on a single income source, and build a resilient and prosperous life.

Chapter 1

Capital Gains

Introduction to Capital Gains

Capital gains represent the profit earned from the sale of an asset that has appreciated in value. Unlike regular income, which is earned through labor or services, capital gains are realized through the increase in the value of investments over time. These gains are a crucial component of wealth building, providing a pathway for significant financial growth and stability.

Capital gains are pivotal in the context of wealth creation for several reasons. They offer the potential for substantial returns, often outpacing other forms of income. Moreover, they provide an opportunity to leverage market dynamics, taking advantage of economic growth and investment trends. Understanding and effectively managing capital gains can significantly enhance one's financial portfolio and long-term wealth.

One of the key advantages of capital gains is their ability to generate higher returns compared to traditional income sources. While wages and salaries are subject to relatively stable and predictable growth, investments in stocks, real estate, or other assets have the potential to appreciate significantly, sometimes exponentially. This appreciation is driven by various factors such as market demand, economic conditions, and company performance, all of which can lead to substantial profits for--- investors.

Furthermore, capital gains offer a degree of flexibility and control that is often not available with regular income. Investors can choose when to sell their assets, allowing them to time their transactions to maximize profits and minimize tax liabilities. This strategic approach to selling assets can be particularly beneficial in optimizing one's overall financial strategy.

Taxation is another important aspect to consider when dealing with capital gains. In many jurisdictions, capital gains are taxed at a lower rate than ordinary income, providing a tax advantage for investors. Long-term capital gains, which are profits from the sale of assets held for more than a year, often enjoy even more favorable tax treatment. This incentivizes long-term investment and can significantly enhance the after-tax returns for investors.

Diversification is also a crucial element in managing capital gains effectively. By spreading investments across different asset classes, sectors, and geographic regions, investors can mitigate risks and increase the likelihood of realizing capital gains. This diversified approach helps protect against market volatility and economic downturns, ensuring a more stable and resilient financial portfolio.

In summary, capital gains play a vital role in wealth creation by offering the potential for higher returns, greater flexibility, and favorable tax treatment. By understanding the dynamics of capital gains and implementing effective investment strategies, individuals can build a robust financial portfolio that supports long-term growth and financial stability.

Types of Capital Gains

Capital gains are broadly categorized into short-term and long-term, based on the duration for which the asset is held before selling.

Short-term Capital Gains

Short-term capital gains are realized from the sale of assets held for less than a year. These gains are typically taxed at the individual's ordinary income tax rate, which can be relatively high. For example, if an investor buys and sells a stock within six months, any profit earned is considered a short-term capital gain. The higher tax rate on short-term gains can significantly impact the net return on investment, making it less attractive for investors who frequently trade assets within a short period.

Long-term Capital Gains

Long-term capital gains, on the other hand, come from assets held for more than a year. These gains benefit from favorable tax rates, which are generally lower than ordinary income tax rates. This distinction encourages investors to hold onto their investments longer, promoting stability and long-term growth. The preferential tax treatment of long-term gains is designed to incentivize long-term investment, which can contribute to economic stability and growth by providing more consistent capital to businesses and markets.

Examples of Assets Generating Capital Gains

Stocks and Equities: Stocks are one of the most common vehicles for capital gains. Investors buy shares in companies, and as these companies grow and succeed, their stock prices typically rise. For instance, an early investment in a technology company like Apple or Amazon has historically yielded substantial capital gains. Shares of companies that appreciate in value over time can generate significant capital gains. For example, if an investor purchases shares of a company at $50 per share and sells them after two years for $100 per share, the $50 profit per share is a long-term capital gain.

Real Estate: Real estate offers another lucrative avenue for capital gains. Investors purchase properties, which can appreciate due to market demand, location, and improvements made to the property. For example, buying a house in an up-and-coming neighborhood and selling it after significant development can result in considerable gains. Properties that increase in market value over time can also generate substantial capital gains. An investor who buys a property for $200,000 and sells it five years later for $300,000 realizes a $100,000 long-term capital gain.

Collectibles: Investments in collectibles such as art, antiques, and rare coins can also yield capital gains. These alternative investments often require specialized knowledge to identify valuable items. For instance, a painting bought for a modest sum could appreciate significantly if the artist gains recognition.

For instance, an art piece bought for $10,000 and sold ten years later for $50,000 results in a $40,000 capital gain.

Mutual Funds and ETFs: Mutual funds and exchange-traded funds (ETFs) provide a diversified approach to investing, pooling money from many investors to buy a variety of assets. These funds can generate capital gains when the underlying assets appreciate in value. An example is a mutual fund focusing on high-growth technology stocks. Pooled investment vehicles like mutual funds and exchange-traded funds (ETFs) can appreciate based on the performance of their underlying assets. If an investor holds shares in a mutual fund for more than a year and the value of those shares increases, the profit realized upon selling is considered a long-term capital gain.

Understanding the differences between short-term and long-term capital gains is essential for effective tax planning and investment strategy. By focusing on long-term investments, investors can take advantage of lower tax rates, which can significantly enhance their overall returns. Additionally, recognizing the types of assets that can generate capital gains allows investors to diversify their portfolios and optimize their potential for financial growth. This strategic approach to investing not only maximizes returns but also promotes financial stability and wealth accumulation over the long term.

Strategies for Maximizing Capital Gains

Maximizing capital gains involves a combination of strategic planning, informed decision-making, and continuous monitoring of the market. Here are some key strategies to consider:

Research and Analysis
Thorough research and analysis are fundamental to maximizing capital gains. Investors need to understand market trends, company performance, and economic indicators. Tools such as fundamental analysis, which evaluates a company's financial

health through metrics like earnings, revenue, and debt levels, and technical analysis, which examines stock price movements and trading volumes, are essential. Utilizing these tools helps investors make informed decisions about which assets to buy, hold, or sell.

- **Fundamental Analysis:** This involves assessing a company's financial statements, management quality, competitive advantages, and market conditions. By understanding the intrinsic value of a company, investors can identify undervalued stocks with high potential for appreciation.
- **Technical Analysis:** This focuses on statistical trends gathered from trading activity, such as price movement and volume. Technical analysis helps in predicting future price movements and identifying optimal entry and exit points for investments.

Timing the Market

While timing the market perfectly is challenging, strategic buying and selling can enhance returns. Investors should look for opportunities to buy undervalued assets and sell when prices peak. This requires staying informed about market cycles, economic news, and company-specific events that can influence asset prices.

- **Market Cycles:** Understanding bull and bear markets can help investors make more strategic decisions. For

example, buying stocks during a market dip and selling during a bull market can maximize gains.
- **Economic Indicators:** Monitoring indicators like interest rates, inflation, and employment rates can provide insights into market conditions and help predict future movements.

Diversification

Diversifying investments across different asset classes and sectors reduces risk and enhances the potential for capital gains. A diversified portfolio might include stocks, real estate, mutual funds, and collectibles, each responding differently to market conditions.

- **Asset Classes:** Including a mix of equities, bonds, real estate, and alternative investments can help spread risk. For instance, when the stock market is down, real estate or bond investments might perform better, balancing overall portfolio performance.
- **Sectors:** Investing in various sectors such as technology, healthcare, finance, and consumer goods ensures that poor performance in one sector does not disproportionately affect the entire portfolio.

Additional Strategies

- **Regular Portfolio Review:** Periodically reviewing and rebalancing the portfolio ensures alignment with

investment goals and market conditions. This might involve selling overperforming assets to lock in gains
- and reinvesting in undervalued opportunities.
- **Tax-efficient Investing:** Utilizing tax-advantaged accounts like IRAs and 401(k)s, and strategically selling assets to offset gains with losses (tax-loss harvesting), can enhance after-tax returns.
- **Long-term Focus:** Prioritizing long-term investments over short-term trades can benefit from compounding returns and favorable long-term capital gains tax rates.

In summary, maximizing capital gains requires a disciplined approach combining thorough research, strategic market timing, diversification, and continuous portfolio management. By employing these strategies, investors can enhance their potential for significant financial growth and long-term wealth accumulation.

Tax Implications and Planning

Effective tax planning is essential for maximizing after-tax returns on investments. Understanding the tax implications of capital gains and employing strategic measures can significantly enhance overall financial outcomes.

Understanding Capital Gains Tax

Capital gains tax is levied on the profit from the sale of assets. The rate at which these gains are taxed depends on the holding period of the asset and the individual's income level.

- **Short-term Capital Gains:** These are gains from the sale of assets held for less than a year and are taxed at the individual's ordinary income tax rate. This rate can be relatively high, depending on the investor's total income.
- **Long-term Capital Gains:** These are gains from assets held for more than a year and are typically taxed at a lower rate. In the U.S., long-term capital gains tax rates can be 0%, 15%, or 20%, depending on the taxpayer's income level. The favorable rates for long-term gains incentivize investors to hold assets for longer periods, promoting more stable investment behavior.

Tax-Efficient Investment Strategies

Investors can employ various strategies to minimize their capital gains tax liability:

- **Tax-Loss Harvesting:** This strategy involves selling investments that are currently at a loss to offset gains from other investments. For example, if an investor has a $10,000 gain from one stock and a $4,000 loss from another, the net taxable gain would be $6,000. This reduces the overall capital gains tax liability.

- **Holding Assets for the Long Term:** By holding investments for more than a year, investors can benefit from the lower long-term capital gains tax rates. This strategy not only reduces tax liability but also allows for the potential growth of investments over time.
- **Strategic Asset Sales:** Timing the sale of assets to coincide with lower income years can help reduce the capital gains tax rate applied. For instance, if an investor expects to have lower income in retirement, deferring the sale of assets until then might result in a lower tax rate on the gains.

Utilizing Tax-Advantaged Accounts

Investing through tax-advantaged accounts can significantly defer or even eliminate capital gains tax, enhancing overall returns.

- **Individual Retirement Accounts (IRAs):** Traditional IRAs allow investments to grow tax-deferred until withdrawals are made, typically in retirement. This deferral can lead to significant growth over time as investments compound without being diminished by taxes. Roth IRAs, on the other hand, offer tax-free growth and tax-free withdrawals for qualified distributions, providing a substantial tax advantage.
- **401(k) Plans:** These employer-sponsored retirement plans also offer tax-deferred growth. Contributions are

made with pre-tax dollars, reducing current taxable income, and investments grow tax-deferred until retirement.
- **Health Savings Accounts (HSAs):** For those with high-deductible health plans, HSAs offer triple tax benefits: contributions are tax-deductible, investments grow tax-deferred, and withdrawals for qualified medical expenses are tax-free.

Additional Considerations
- **Capital Gains Exclusion for Primary Residences:** In the U.S., individuals can exclude up to $250,000 ($500,000 for married couples) of capital gains on the sale of a primary residence, provided certain conditions are met. This exclusion can significantly reduce tax liability on real estate gains.
- **Gift and Estate Planning:** Gifting appreciated assets to family members in lower tax brackets or donating them to charity can minimize capital gains taxes. Additionally, assets inherited receive a step-up in basis, potentially eliminating capital gains tax on appreciation during the original owner's lifetime.

Case Studies

Understanding real-world examples can provide valuable insights into successful investment strategies and the potential for capital gains across different asset classes. Here are some detailed case studies:

Successful Stock Investments

Consider the case of John, who invested $10,000 in Amazon stock in the early 2000s. Recognizing the company's innovative potential and its position in the burgeoning e-commerce market, John decided to hold onto his investment for over a decade. As Amazon expanded its services, diversified its offerings, and grew its customer base, the company's stock price experienced exponential growth. By the end of his holding period, the value of John's investment had soared to hundreds of thousands of dollars, resulting in substantial long-term capital gains far exceeding his initial investment. This example illustrates the power of long-term investment and the significant wealth-building potential of identifying and investing in high-growth companies early on.

Profitable Real Estate Flips

Emily, a real estate investor, bought a rundown property in a growing neighborhood for $150,000. Recognizing the area's potential for appreciation, she invested an additional $50,000 in renovations, transforming the property into a desirable home. Two years later, Emily sold the property for $300,000, realizing a significant capital gain of $100,000 after accounting for her total investment. Her decision to hold the property for more than a year allowed her to benefit from favorable long-term capital gains tax rates. This case study highlights the potential for substantial profits through strategic real estate investments, particularly when improvements are made to enhance the property's value.

High-Return Alternative Investments

Sarah, an art collector with a keen eye for emerging talent, purchased a painting by a then-unknown artist for $5,000. Over the years, as the artist gained recognition and acclaim, the painting's value increased significantly. When Sarah eventually sold the painting for $50,000, she achieved a substantial capital gain of $45,000. This case exemplifies the potential of alternative investments, such as art, to deliver high returns. It also underscores the importance of patience and holding onto assets as they appreciate in value over time.

Additional Case Studies

Strategic Diversification

David, a diversified investor, spread his investments across various asset classes, including stocks, real estate, mutual funds, and precious metals. By diversifying his portfolio, David mitigated risks and maximized his potential for capital gains. During economic downturns, while his stock investments might have underperformed, his real estate and precious metal holdings provided stability and continued appreciation. This strategic diversification allowed David to maintain steady growth in his portfolio, demonstrating the benefits of spreading investments across different asset classes.

Tax-Efficient Retirement Savings

Linda, a diligent saver, maximized her contributions to her 401(k) and Roth IRA accounts. By doing so, she deferred taxes on her 401(k) investments and enjoyed tax-free growth and withdrawals from her Roth IRA. Over several decades, her consistent contributions and the compounding growth of her investments led to a substantial retirement nest egg. Linda's case illustrates the power of tax-advantaged accounts in building wealth and minimizing tax liabilities on capital gains.

Real Estate Development

Mark, a seasoned real estate developer, purchased a large plot of land in an underdeveloped area. Over the next five years, he developed the land into a residential community, complete with modern amenities and infrastructure. By the time he sold the developed properties, the area's demand had surged, resulting in significant capital gains. Mark's foresight and long-term planning not only yielded high returns but also benefited from favorable long-term capital gains tax rates.

In summary, these case studies demonstrate the diverse ways investors can achieve significant capital gains through strategic investments in stocks, real estate, alternative assets, and diversified portfolios. They also highlight the importance of understanding market dynamics, tax implications, and the benefits of long-term investment horizons in maximizing financial growth and stability.

Risks and Mitigation

Investing for capital gains involves inherent risks that can affect the value of investments. Understanding these risks and implementing strategies to mitigate them is crucial for protecting and growing one's portfolio.

Market Volatility
Capital gains investments are highly susceptible to market fluctuations. Stocks can lose value due to economic downturns, geopolitical events, or changes in company performance. Similarly, real estate prices can decline due to economic conditions, changes in interest rates, or local market dynamics.

- **Mitigation Strategy:** Diversification and a long-term perspective are key to mitigating these risks. By spreading investments across various asset classes, sectors, and geographic regions, investors can reduce the impact of volatility in any one area. Additionally, maintaining a long-term investment horizon allows for the smoothing out of short-term market fluctuations and capitalizing on overall market growth over time.

Liquidity Risks

Some investments, such as real estate and collectibles, can be less liquid than stocks, meaning they cannot be quickly converted to cash. This can pose a challenge if an investor needs immediate access to funds.

- **Mitigation Strategy:** Balancing portfolios with both liquid (e.g., stocks, bonds) and illiquid assets (e.g., real estate, art) helps maintain financial flexibility. Having a mix of asset types ensures that investors can access cash when needed without being forced to sell illiquid investments at an unfavorable time.

Mitigation Strategies

Diversification

Diversification involves spreading investments across various asset classes, sectors, and geographic regions to reduce risk.

- **Example:** An investor might allocate funds to a mix of stocks, bonds, real estate, and alternative investments like commodities or art. This approach minimizes the impact of poor performance in any single investment category.

Research

Continuous research and monitoring of market trends are essential for making informed investment decisions. Staying updated on economic indicators, industry developments, and company performance helps investors adjust their strategies accordingly.

- **Example:** An investor regularly reviews financial news, company reports, and economic forecasts to stay informed about potential risks and opportunities. This proactive approach enables timely adjustments to the investment portfolio.

Professional Advice

Consulting financial advisors or investment professionals can provide valuable insights and expertise. Advisors can help in crafting personalized investment strategies, identifying risks, and suggesting appropriate mitigation measures.

- **Example:** An investor works with a financial advisor to develop a diversified investment plan, periodically reviews the portfolio's performance, and makes adjustments based on the advisor's recommendations. This collaboration ensures that the investor's strategies are aligned with their financial goals and risk tolerance.

Interest Rate Risks

Changes in interest rates can significantly impact investments, particularly in bonds and real estate. Rising interest rates can lead to lower bond prices and higher mortgage costs, affecting the value of these investments.

- **Mitigation Strategy:** Diversifying across different bond maturities and including variable rate instruments can help manage interest rate risk. Additionally, investing in real estate with fixed-rate mortgages can protect against rising rates.

Inflation Risks

Inflation can erode the purchasing power of investment returns. Investments that do not keep pace with inflation can result in a real loss of value over time.

- **Mitigation Strategy:** Investing in assets that historically outpace inflation, such as stocks, real estate, and commodities, can help preserve purchasing power. Including Treasury Inflation-Protected Securities (TIPS) in a portfolio can also provide a hedge against inflation.

Regulatory Risks

Changes in regulations and tax laws can impact the performance and attractiveness of certain investments. For example, new tax policies can affect capital gains taxation or specific industry regulations can influence market dynamics.

- **Mitigation Strategy:** Staying informed about potential regulatory changes and adjusting investment strategies accordingly is essential. Consulting with tax professionals and legal advisors can help navigate complex regulatory environments and identify potential impacts on investments.

In summary, while investing for capital gains involves various risks, implementing effective mitigation strategies can help protect and grow one's portfolio. Diversification, continuous research, professional advice, and a balanced approach to liquidity and risk management are crucial components of a successful investment strategy. By understanding and addressing these risks, investors can enhance their potential for achieving long-term financial growth and stability.

Conclusion

Capital gains are a powerful engine for wealth creation, offering the potential for substantial returns through strategic investment. By understanding the types of capital gains, employing effective strategies, and being mindful of tax implications, investors can maximize their wealth-building potential. Real-life case studies highlight the success that can be achieved, while awareness of risks ensures a balanced approach. As the first chapter of "7 Streams of wealth," capital gains lay the foundation for a diversified and resilient financial portfolio, guiding readers on the path to long-term wealth and financial independence.

Maximizing Wealth Through Capital Gains

Capital gains represent one of the most effective avenues for generating significant wealth. By investing in appreciating assets like stocks, real estate, and alternative investments, individuals can realize substantial returns over time. The potential for high returns makes capital gains an essential component of any comprehensive wealth-building strategy.

Understanding Capital Gains

Capital gains are classified into short-term and long-term categories, each with distinct characteristics and tax implications. Short-term capital gains are realized from assets held for less than a year and are taxed at the investor's ordinary income rate, which can be relatively high. Long-term capital gains, from assets held for more than a year, enjoy favorable tax treatment, often at lower rates. This distinction underscores the importance of a long-term investment perspective to maximize after-tax returns.

Effective Strategies for Capital Gains

To maximize capital gains, investors should consider employing several key strategies:

- **Research and Analysis:** Thoroughly researching potential investments and understanding market trends, company performance, and economic indicators can lead to more informed and profitable decisions.
- **Market Timing:** While timing the market perfectly is challenging, strategic buying during market dips and selling during peaks can enhance returns.
- **Diversification:** Spreading investments across different asset classes and sectors reduces risk and enhances potential gains. A well-diversified portfolio might include a mix of stocks, bonds, real estate, and alternative investments.
- **Tax-Efficient Investment:** Utilizing tax-advantaged accounts, such as IRAs and 401(k)s, and strategies like tax-loss harvesting can significantly reduce tax liabilities and improve net returns.

Real-Life Case Studies

Real-life examples illustrate the success that can be achieved through strategic investment in capital gains:
- **Successful Stock Investments:** Investing in high-growth companies and holding for the long term can result in substantial gains. For example, early investors in tech giants like Amazon or Apple have seen their investments grow exponentially.

- **Profitable Real Estate Flips:** Strategic purchases and renovations in growing neighborhoods can lead to significant profits, as seen in the case of Emily, who transformed a rundown property into a lucrative sale.
- **High-Return Alternative Investments:** Investing in undervalued art or collectibles and holding until their value appreciates can yield impressive returns, as demonstrated by Sarah's art investment.

Awareness of Risks

While the potential for capital gains is significant, being aware of and mitigating risks is crucial for maintaining a balanced investment approach:

- **Market Volatility:** Diversification and a long-term investment horizon help manage the impact of market fluctuations.
- **Liquidity Risks:** Balancing portfolios with both liquid and illiquid assets ensures financial flexibility.
- **Interest Rate and Inflation Risks:** Diversifying across different bond maturities and including inflation-protected securities can help manage these risks.
- **Regulatory Risks:** Staying informed about regulatory changes and consulting with professionals can navigate potential impacts on investments.

Building a Diversified Financial Portfolio

As the first chapter of "7 Streams of Income," capital gains form a critical foundation for a diversified and resilient financial portfolio. By integrating capital gains with other income streams, such as dividends, rental income, and business income, investors can create a robust financial strategy that enhances overall stability and growth potential.

Path to Financial Independence

Strategic investment in capital gains, combined with a comprehensive understanding of the associated risks and tax implications, sets the stage for long-term wealth creation. By leveraging effective strategies and learning from real-life case studies, investors can build a diversified portfolio that not only generates significant returns but also guides them toward financial independence and security.

Chapter 2

Interest Income

Introduction to Interest Income

Interest income represents the earnings generated from lending money or investing in interest-bearing financial instruments such as savings accounts, certificates of deposit (CDs), bonds, and other fixed-income securities. This type of income is distinct from capital gains, which are profits realized from the appreciation of an asset's value over time. Unlike capital gains, interest income provides a steady and predictable stream of revenue, contributing to financial stability and growth.

Interest income plays a crucial role in wealth building due to its relatively low-risk and stable return on investment. It is a key component in diversifying an income portfolio, particularly because it often remains consistent even during market fluctuations. This characteristic of stability makes interest income an attractive option for conservative investors and those looking to balance more volatile income streams, such as stock dividends or capital gains from equity investments.

Understanding the various sources of interest income is essential for optimizing one's financial strategy. Common sources include:

1. **Savings Accounts:** While savings accounts typically offer lower interest rates compared to other instruments, they provide high liquidity and security.
2. **Certificates of Deposit (CDs):** CDs generally offer higher interest rates than savings accounts in exchange for locking in the investment for a fixed period. This makes them suitable for those who can afford to set aside funds without immediate access.
3. **Bonds:** Investing in government, municipal, or corporate bonds can yield higher interest income, depending on the creditworthiness of the issuer and the bond's duration. Bonds can be an excellent way to earn interest while diversifying risk.
4. **Money Market Accounts:** These accounts offer a higher interest rate than regular savings accounts and provide a good balance between yield and liquidity.

Maximizing returns on interest income involves strategic planning and awareness of market conditions. Here are a few tips to enhance interest income:

- **Laddering Investments:** This strategy involves spreading investments across multiple instruments with varying maturity dates, ensuring regular income and reducing interest rate risk.
- **Monitoring Interest Rates:** Keeping an eye on interest rate trends can help in making timely adjustments to

your investment portfolio to take advantage of higher rates.
- **Diversifying Sources:** Investing in a mix of interest-bearing instruments can spread risk and optimize returns.

Interest income is not only a cornerstone for conservative investment strategies but also a vital part of a well-rounded financial plan. By leveraging interest-bearing instruments, investors can secure a reliable income stream that supports long-term financial goals and stability.

Types of Interest Income

Interest income can be derived from several types of financial instruments, each with its unique characteristics and potential returns. Understanding these various sources can help investors choose the best options for their financial goals and risk tolerance.

Savings Accounts

Savings accounts are one of the most straightforward and accessible sources of interest income. Banks offer interest on the deposited amount, providing a safe and liquid investment option. Although the interest rates are typically lower compared to other instruments, savings accounts offer unparalleled security and ease of access. They are ideal for emergency funds or short-term savings goals due to their high liquidity and virtually no risk of losing the principal amount.

Certificates of Deposit (CDs)

Certificates of Deposit (CDs) are time deposits offered by banks that pay a fixed interest rate over a specified period. They usually offer higher interest rates than regular savings accounts in exchange for locking up the funds for the term of the CD. For instance, a five-year CD might offer a significantly higher interest rate than a one-year CD, rewarding the investor for the longer commitment. CDs are a suitable option for those who can afford to set aside funds without needing immediate access, providing a balance of higher returns and low risk.

Bonds

Bonds are debt securities issued by governments, municipalities, or corporations to raise capital. Investors who purchase bonds receive periodic interest payments (coupon payments) and the return of the principal amount at maturity. Bonds vary in terms of risk and return:

- **Government Bonds:** Typically offer lower returns but higher safety, as they are backed by the issuing government.
- **Municipal Bonds:** Issued by municipalities, these can offer tax advantages in addition to interest income.

- **Corporate Bonds:** Usually offer higher returns compared to government bonds but come with higher risk, depending on the issuing corporation's creditworthiness.

Bonds are a versatile option for investors seeking regular income and are often used to diversify a portfolio.

Peer-to-Peer Lending

Peer-to-peer (P2P) lending platforms connect borrowers with individual lenders, offering potentially higher interest rates than traditional savings accounts or CDs. These platforms enable investors to fund personal loans, small business loans, or other types of credit, earning interest on the amounts lent. While P2P lending can provide higher returns, it also carries higher risks, including the potential for borrower default. Investors must carefully assess the credit risk associated with each loan and consider diversifying their P2P lending investments to mitigate risk.

Money Market Accounts

Money market accounts combine features of savings accounts and checking accounts, typically offering higher interest rates than regular savings accounts. They provide a good balance between yield and liquidity, making them an attractive option for those who need regular access to their funds while still earning a reasonable interest rate.

Treasury Securities

Treasury securities, including Treasury bills (T-bills), Treasury notes (T-notes), and Treasury bonds (T-bonds), are issued by the federal government and are considered one of the safest investments. T-bills are short-term securities with maturities of one year or less, T-notes have maturities ranging from two to ten years, and T-bonds have maturities of more than ten years. These securities provide interest income through periodic coupon payments and are highly secure, making them suitable for risk-averse investors.

Real Estate Investment Trusts (REITs)

Although not a traditional interest-bearing instrument, Real Estate Investment Trusts (REITs) offer another way to earn income. REITs own and manage income-generating real estate properties and distribute the majority of their earnings to shareholders as dividends. While REITs can offer attractive yields, they also come with market risk and are influenced by real estate market conditions.

Maximizing Interest Income

Maximizing interest income involves strategic planning and

understanding key principles that influence returns on interest-bearing investments. Here are essential strategies to optimize interest income:

Understanding Interest Rates

Interest rates are fundamental to the returns on interest-bearing investments. Higher interest rates generally lead to higher returns, but they also signify increased risk in certain investments. It's crucial for investors to stay informed about the prevailing interest rate environment and adapt their investment strategies accordingly. For example, during periods of rising interest rates, locking in rates with long-term CDs or bonds can be advantageous as it secures higher yields over the investment period.

Diversifying Interest-Bearing Investments

Diversification is paramount for managing risk and enhancing returns. By spreading investments across various interest-bearing instruments, investors can mitigate the volatility and risk associated with any single investment. A well-diversified portfolio might include a blend of:

- **Savings Accounts:** Offering liquidity and security with lower but stable returns.
- **Certificates of Deposit (CDs):** Providing higher yields for fixed periods, rewarding investors for locking in funds.

- **Bonds:** Offering varying risk levels and returns based on issuer creditworthiness and maturity.
- **Peer-to-Peer (P2P) Lending:** Potentially yielding higher returns but carrying higher risk due to borrower default possibilities.

This diversified approach balances high-yield opportunities with safer, lower-yield options, ensuring a stable and consistent income stream.

Reinvestment and Compounding

Reinvesting interest income is a powerful strategy for accelerating wealth accumulation through compounding. Compounding occurs when earned interest is reinvested into additional interest-bearing investments, generating returns on both the original principal and previously earned interest. Over time, this compounding effect can significantly enhance overall returns. For instance, dividends from stocks or interest from bonds can be reinvested to purchase more shares or bonds, thereby magnifying the investment's growth potential exponentially.

Tax Considerations

Understanding the tax implications of interest income is vital for maximizing net returns. Different types of interest-bearing investments may have varying tax treatments, such as taxable interest from CDs or bonds versus tax-free interest from municipal bonds. Investors should consider tax-efficient strategies to minimize tax liabilities and optimize after-tax returns.

Monitoring and Adjusting

Regularly monitoring the performance of interest-bearing investments and adjusting the portfolio as needed is crucial for maximizing income. Economic conditions, interest rate movements, and changes in personal financial goals should all prompt adjustments to ensure the portfolio remains aligned with desired risk levels and income objectives.

Tax Implications and Strategies for Interest Income

Tax Treatment of Interest Income

Interest income is typically taxed as ordinary income. The specific tax rate applied to this income depends on the investor's overall income and tax bracket. Understanding these tax implications is crucial for effective financial planning and maximizing net returns. For instance, higher-income individuals may face a higher marginal tax rate on their interest income compared to those in lower tax brackets.

Tax-Advantaged Accounts

Utilizing tax-advantaged accounts can be an effective strategy for managing taxes on interest income. Two common types of such accounts are Individual Retirement Accounts (IRAs) and 401(k) plans.

- **Traditional IRA**: Interest earned within a Traditional IRA is tax-deferred, meaning you won't pay taxes on this income until you withdraw it, typically during retirement. This deferral can help manage tax liability during your earning years and potentially lower your tax rate upon withdrawal if your income is lower in retirement.
- **Roth IRA**: Interest earned within a Roth IRA grows tax-free. Qualified withdrawals from a Roth IRA are also tax-free, providing a significant tax advantage if certain conditions are met, such as the account being open for at least five years and the account holder being at least 59½ years old.
- **401(k) Plans**: Similar to IRAs, 401(k) plans offer tax-deferred growth on interest income. Contributions to a traditional 401(k) are made pre-tax, reducing your taxable income in the year of contribution. The interest income and other earnings within the account are taxed upon withdrawal.

Strategies for Minimizing Tax Liability

Investors can employ various strategies to minimize their tax liability on interest income. Some of the most effective strategies include:

- **Municipal Bonds**: Interest earned from municipal bonds is often exempt from federal income tax. Additionally, if you purchase bonds issued by your state or local government, the interest income may also be exempt from state and local taxes. This makes municipal bonds an attractive option for investors in higher tax brackets.
- **Laddering CDs and Bonds**: Creating a ladder of Certificates of Deposit (CDs) or bonds involves purchasing these instruments with different maturity dates. This strategy can help manage tax impacts by spreading out the income over several years, potentially keeping you in a lower tax bracket. Additionally, laddering provides more consistent cash flow and reduces the risk of having to reinvest all your funds at once, possibly in a less favorable interest rate environment.
- **Tax-Loss Harvesting**: This strategy involves selling investments that have declined in value to offset the interest income and other gains. By realizing these losses, you can reduce your taxable income. It's important to be mindful of the IRS wash-sale rule, which

prohibits repurchasing the same or substantially identical security within 30 days before or after the sale.

Case Studies: Successful Strategies in Interest-Bearing Investments

Successful Savings Accounts

Consider Jane, an individual who makes it a habit to regularly deposit money into a high-yield savings account. Unlike many who settle for traditional savings accounts offering a meager 0.1% interest, Jane opts for an online bank that provides a 2% interest rate. This decision significantly enhances her interest income. Over ten years, Jane's consistent deposits, combined with the power of compounding interest, result in substantial growth in her savings. By the end of this period, she has not only built a secure financial cushion but also maximized her interest earnings, demonstrating the impact of choosing higher-yielding savings options.

Profitable Bond Investments

Mike, a conservative investor, allocates a portion of his portfolio to U.S. Treasury bonds. He employs a strategy known as bond laddering, where he purchases bonds with varying maturities. This approach provides regular interest payments and minimizes reinvestment risk, as the bonds mature at different times, allowing Mike to reinvest at potentially higher rates if interest rates rise. His strategy ensures a stable income stream while preserving capital, showcasing the reliability and importance of bonds in a well-rounded investment portfolio.

High-Yield Peer-to-Peer Lending

Sarah, an investor with a higher risk tolerance, ventures into peer-to-peer (P2P) lending. She diversifies her investments across multiple borrowers with varying credit profiles, enabling her to earn higher interest rates compared to traditional savings accounts. Although some loans do default, the overall return on her diversified P2P portfolio exceeds that of safer investments. Sarah's approach illustrates the potential for higher yields through careful risk management and diversification in the P2P lending market.

Risks and Mitigation Strategies

Inflation Risk

Inflation risk is the danger that the purchasing power of money will decline over time due to rising prices, potentially diminishing the real returns on interest-bearing investments. To mitigate this risk, investors can seek higher-yielding instruments or those that offer inflation protection. One such option is Treasury Inflation-Protected Securities (TIPS), which adjust the principal value in line with inflation, thereby safeguarding real returns.

Credit Risk

Credit risk refers to the possibility of a borrower defaulting on a loan or bond, leading to potential losses for the investor. To reduce credit risk, investors can focus on high-quality bonds, such as U.S. Treasuries, which are backed by the full faith and credit of the U.S. government. Additionally, diversifying investments across multiple issuers and sectors can further mitigate the impact of any single default, spreading the risk and protecting the portfolio.

Interest Rate Risk

Interest rate risk arises from fluctuations in interest rates, which can affect the value of fixed-income investments. For example, rising interest rates generally lead to declining bond prices. To manage this risk, investors can diversify their bond holdings across different maturities, creating a bond ladder. This strategy helps spread out the impact of interest rate changes. Additionally, avoiding long-term bonds during periods of expected rate increases can prevent locking in lower rates for extended periods, thereby reducing potential losses.

Conclusion

Interest income provides a stable and predictable stream of revenue, essential for diversifying an income portfolio and achieving long-term financial goals. By understanding the various sources of interest income, employing strategies to maximize returns, and being mindful of tax implications and risks, investors can effectively leverage interest income to build and sustain wealth. Real-life case studies illustrate the potential for success, while risk mitigation ensures a balanced and resilient approach. As the second chapter of "7 Streams of Wealth," interest income highlights the importance of steady, low-risk investments in a comprehensive wealth-building strategy, guiding readers towards financial security and growt

Chapter 3

Earned Income

1. Introduction to Earned Income

Earned income refers to the money received in exchange for performing work or services. This type of income is the result of active effort, be it through traditional employment, freelancing, or running a business. For most individuals, earned income is the primary source of financial support and a key component of their overall income strategy. It is the cornerstone upon which wealth-building is often based, as it provides the necessary capital to invest in other income-generating activities.

Unlike passive income streams such as dividends or rental income, earned income requires continuous effort and time commitment. Therefore, maximizing earned income involves enhancing one's skills, optimizing job opportunities, and strategically managing career growth. A strong understanding of how to effectively generate and increase earned income is essential for achieving financial stability and long-term wealth.

2. Traditional Employment

Traditional employment is a fundamental source of earned income for many individuals. This form of employment offers a structured environment with defined roles and responsibilities. It typically involves working for an employer who provides a regular paycheck, along with various benefits.

Full-time vs Part-time Work

- **Full-time Employment:** Full-time jobs generally offer higher salaries and more comprehensive benefits compared to part-time roles. These benefits often include health insurance, retirement plans, paid time off, and job security. Full-time positions typically require a commitment of around 35-40 hours per week, providing a stable and predictable income stream.
- **Part-time Employment:** Part-time jobs offer greater flexibility, making them suitable for individuals who need to balance work with other commitments such as education or family responsibilities. However, part-time roles usually come with fewer benefits and lower pay. Despite this, part-time work can be a valuable source of earned income, especially when combined with other income streams or as a means to gain experience and skills.

Benefits and Drawbacks of Traditional Employment

- **Benefits:**
    - **Stability:** Regular paychecks provide financial

- security and predictability, making it easier to plan and manage personal finances.
- **Benefits Packages:** Access to health insurance, retirement plans, and other employee benefits can significantly enhance financial well-being.
- **Career Development:** Many employers offer opportunities for professional growth, including training programs, promotions, and career advancement paths.

- **Drawbacks:**
    - **Limited Earning Potential:** Salaries and wages in traditional employment are often capped, limiting the potential for significant income increases without changing roles or employers.
    - **Lack of Flexibility:** Full-time jobs can be demanding and leave little room for personal pursuits or additional income-generating activities.
    - **Job Satisfaction:** Not all jobs offer personal fulfillment, and some may find traditional employment monotonous or unchallenging.

Salary Negotiation and Job Market Trends

Negotiating your salary is a crucial skill for maximizing earned income. Understanding the current job market trends and industry standards is essential for effective negotiation.

- **Research and Preparation:** Before entering salary negotiations, gather information on typical salaries for your role and industry. Websites like Glassdoor, PayScale, and industry reports can provide valuable data.
- **Highlight Your Value:** Emphasize your skills, experience, and accomplishments that make you a valuable asset to the company. Demonstrating your contributions and potential can strengthen your negotiating position.
- **Consider the Whole Package:** Evaluate the entire compensation package, including benefits, bonuses, and non-monetary perks. Sometimes, improving benefits or work conditions can be as valuable as a salary increase.

Job Market Trends:

- **Tech Industry Boom:** With the rapid growth of the tech sector, professionals in fields like software development, data analysis, and cybersecurity are in high demand, often commanding higher salaries and attractive benefits.
- **Remote Work:** The rise of remote work has broadened job opportunities, allowing individuals to work for companies outside their geographic area, often with flexible schedules and reduced commuting costs.

- **Healthcare Demand:** The healthcare industry continues to grow, driven by an aging population and increased focus on health and wellness. This trend creates opportunities for well-paying roles in various healthcare professions.

3. Freelancing and Gig Economy

The gig economy has revolutionized the way people work, providing opportunities to earn income through short-term contracts and freelance projects. Digital platforms like Upwork, Fiverr, and Uber have made it easier than ever to find freelance work, enabling individuals to leverage their skills and talents outside the confines of traditional employment.

Definition and Growth

Freelancing involves working on a per-project basis rather than being permanently employed by a single company. It allows for flexibility and independence, attracting those who prefer non-traditional work arrangements. The gig economy, a broader term encompassing various forms of temporary and freelance work, has experienced rapid growth driven by several key factors:
- **Technological Advancements:** The internet and digital platforms have facilitated the connection between

freelancers and clients worldwide. These technologies enable remote work, online collaboration, and digital payments, making freelancing more accessible and efficient.

- **Shifting Work Preferences:** Many workers now prioritize work-life balance, autonomy, and the ability to pursue diverse interests. Freelancing offers the flexibility to choose projects, set working hours, and work from different locations.
- **Economic Trends:** Companies are increasingly outsourcing tasks to freelancers to reduce overhead costs and gain access to specialized skills as needed. This trend has expanded the demand for freelance services across various industries.

The gig economy's rapid growth is evident in its numbers. According to a report by Upwork, the number of freelancers in the United States alone reached 59 million in 2020, contributing $1.2 trillion to the economy. This shift indicates a significant transformation in how work is structured and delivered.

Pros and Cons

Freelancing offers numerous advantages but also presents unique challenges that must be managed effectively.

- **Pros:**
  - **Flexibility:** Freelancers can set their schedules, choose their projects, and work from virtually anywhere. This flexibility can lead to a better work-life balance and increased job satisfaction.
  - **Independence:** Freelancers have the autonomy to select projects that align with their skills and interests. They can diversify their income by working with multiple clients and exploring different fields.
  - **Potential for Higher Earnings:** Skilled freelancers can often command higher rates than traditional employees, especially for specialized or high-demand services.

- **Cons:**
  - **Income Instability:** Freelancers may face fluctuating income levels due to the project-based nature of their work. This instability can make financial planning challenging.
  - **Lack of Benefits:** Unlike traditional employees, freelancers do not receive benefits such as health insurance, retirement plans, or paid leave. They must manage these aspects independently.
  - **Workload Management:** Successful freelancing requires juggling multiple clients

and projects simultaneously. Effective time management and organizational skills are crucial to meeting deadlines and maintaining quality.

Platforms and Opportunities

Freelancers can find opportunities across a wide range of fields, from creative and technical services to consulting and manual labor. Key platforms and their specific niches include:

- **Upwork:** A comprehensive platform that connects freelancers with clients across various industries, including writing, design, marketing, and IT.
- **Fiverr:** Known for its gig-based system, Fiverr allows freelancers to offer specific services at set prices, catering to creative fields like graphic design, writing, and digital marketing.
- **Uber and Lyft:** These ride-sharing platforms offer opportunities for individuals to earn income by providing transportation services.
- **TaskRabbit:** This platform connects freelancers with clients needing help with tasks like moving, cleaning, and home repairs.

Building a successful freelance career involves several key strategies:

- **Building a Strong Portfolio:** A compelling portfolio showcasing past work and success stories can attract potential clients and demonstrate expertise.
- **Leveraging Platforms:** Actively using freelance platforms to find and apply for relevant projects can increase visibility and opportunities.
- **Networking:** Connecting with other freelancers and industry professionals can lead to referrals and collaborative opportunities.

4. Entrepreneurship and Small Businesses

Starting a business can be a highly rewarding way to generate earned income. Entrepreneurs have the potential to turn their ideas into profitable ventures, but it requires dedication, resilience, and strategic planning. Entrepreneurship offers the chance to create something from the ground up, provide value to customers, and achieve financial independence.

Starting Your Own Business

Launching a business involves several crucial steps, each of which requires careful consideration and planning:
- **Market Research:** This is the foundation of any successful business. Understanding the target market, identifying customer needs, and analyzing competitors are essential to finding a viable business idea. Market

research helps in understanding demand, pricing strategies, and potential barriers to entry.

- **Business Planning:** A comprehensive business plan outlines the business goals, strategies for achieving them, and the roadmap for growth. It includes details on the business model, marketing strategies, financial projections, and operational plans. A well-thought-out business plan can also help attract investors and secure funding.
- **Securing Funding:** Starting a business often requires capital. Entrepreneurs can seek funding through various sources, including personal savings, loans, investors, or crowdfunding. Understanding the financial needs of the business and preparing to pitch to potential investors is crucial.
- **Identifying a Niche Market:** Focusing on a niche market can provide a competitive advantage. By catering to a specific group of customers with unique needs, a business can differentiate itself from competitors and build a loyal customer base.

Challenges and Rewards

Entrepreneurship comes with significant challenges and rewards. Understanding these can help aspiring entrepreneurs prepare for the journey ahead:

- **Challenges:**

- **Financial Uncertainty:** Unlike traditional employment, starting a business often involves financial risks. Initial investment costs, variable income, and the possibility of business failure can create financial uncertainty.
- **Long Working Hours:** Building a business from scratch requires considerable time and effort. Entrepreneurs often work long hours, especially in the early stages, to establish their business.
- **Stress and Pressure:** The responsibility of running a business, managing employees, and meeting customer expectations can be stressful. Entrepreneurs must be resilient and able to handle pressure.

- **Rewards:**
  - **High Rewards:** Successful businesses can generate significant financial returns, offering the potential for high income and financial independence.
  - **Personal Fulfillment:** Creating a business that provides value to customers and contributes to the community can be deeply fulfilling. The sense of accomplishment from building

something from the ground up is a major reward for many entrepreneurs.
- **Autonomy and Control:** Entrepreneurs have the freedom to make decisions and shape the direction of their business. This autonomy allows for creativity and innovation.

Case Studies

Consider the story of Sarah, who started a homemade soap business. Initially, Sarah made soap as a hobby. She began selling her products at local craft fairs and through social media marketing. Her unique recipes and eco-friendly packaging resonated with customers, leading to increased demand. Sarah then expanded her business to online sales and wholesale distribution. Through dedication and strategic marketing, she turned her passion into a profitable venture, illustrating the potential of entrepreneurship.

5. Consulting and Professional Services

Consulting offers another avenue for earning income by leveraging your expertise to help businesses improve their operations. It allows professionals to provide valuable advice and solutions to organizations seeking to enhance their performance.

Types of Consulting Work

Consulting can encompass a wide range of services, each requiring specific skills and knowledge:

- **Management Consulting:** Focuses on improving organizational performance, strategy development, and operational efficiency.
- **IT Consulting:** Involves advising on technology solutions, system implementation, and cybersecurity measures.
- **Marketing Consulting:** Provides expertise in market research, branding, and digital marketing strategies.
- **Financial Consulting:** Offers guidance on financial planning, investment strategies, and risk management.

Building a Consulting Business

To succeed as a consultant, it's essential to establish credibility, network effectively, and continuously update your skills:

- **Establish Credibility:** Building a strong reputation in your field is crucial. This can be achieved through professional certifications, publishing articles, and speaking at industry events.
- **Networking:** Connecting with industry professionals, attending conferences, and joining professional associations can help generate referrals and new business opportunities.

- **Online Presence:** A professional website, active social media profiles, and client testimonials can enhance your visibility and attract potential clients.

Success Stories

John, a former corporate executive, transitioned to consulting after identifying a demand for his expertise in organizational restructuring. By focusing on small to medium-sized businesses, he built a successful consulting practice. John's deep industry knowledge and strategic approach allowed him to provide valuable insights, leading to significant improvements for his clients.

6. Side Hustles

Side hustles provide an additional income stream alongside your primary job. They offer a way to pursue passions, develop new skills, or simply boost earnings.

Definition and Examples

Common side hustles include:
- **Blogging:** Creating content on topics of interest and monetizing through ads, sponsorships, and affiliate marketing.
- **Tutoring:** Offering educational assistance in subjects like math, science, or languages, either in person or online.

- **Selling Handmade Crafts:** Producing and selling handmade items such as jewelry, clothing, or home decor on platforms like Etsy.

Balancing with a Full-time Job

Managing a side hustle requires effective time management. Here are some strategies:

- **Set Clear Boundaries:** Allocate specific time slots for your side hustle to ensure it doesn't interfere with your primary job or personal life.
- **Prioritize Tasks:** Focus on high-impact activities that generate the most income or progress.
- **Delegate:** Where possible, outsource tasks that can be handled by others to free up your time for more critical aspects of your side hustle.

Case Studies

Lisa, a full-time teacher, started a tutoring business to supplement her income. By offering online sessions and specializing in math, she grew her side hustle into a significant source of additional income. Lisa's expertise and flexible scheduling attracted many students, and her personalized approach led to high satisfaction rates. Over time, her tutoring business became a reliable and rewarding income stream.

7. Increasing Your Earned Income

Maximizing earned income involves strategic career planning and continuous improvement. Here are key strategies to boost your earning potential:

Career Advancement

Pursuing promotions and new opportunities within your field can significantly increase your earning potential. Career advancement is often tied to professional development and networking. Here are some steps to consider:

- **Set Career Goals:** Define short-term and long-term career goals. This clarity helps you stay focused and motivated.
- **Seek Promotions:** Demonstrate your value to your employer by exceeding expectations, taking on additional responsibilities, and showcasing your achievements.
- **Explore New Opportunities:** If advancement within your current organization is limited, consider seeking opportunities elsewhere. Changing companies can sometimes result in significant salary increases.
- **Professional Development:** Continuously improve your skills and knowledge. Attend workshops, seminars, and

conferences related to your field. Stay updated on industry trends and best practices.

Continuing Education and Skill Development

Investing in further education, such as obtaining certifications or advanced degrees, can enhance your qualifications and open up higher-paying roles:

- **Advanced Degrees:** Pursuing a master's degree or doctorate can qualify you for specialized, higher-paying positions in your field.
- **Certifications:** Many industries offer certifications that can enhance your credibility and expertise. For example, obtaining a Project Management Professional (PMP) certification can lead to higher-paying roles in project management.
- **Online Courses:** Utilize online learning platforms like Coursera, Udemy, and LinkedIn Learning to acquire new skills and stay competitive in the job market.

Networking and Personal Branding

Building a professional network and establishing a strong personal brand can lead to new opportunities and higher earning potential. Social media and industry events are valuable tools for networking:

- **Professional Networking:** Attend industry conferences, seminars, and local meetups to connect with other professionals in your field. Join professional associations and online forums.
- **Mentorship:** Seek out mentors who can provide guidance, advice, and introductions to influential people in your industry.
- **Personal Branding:** Establish a strong online presence by creating a professional LinkedIn profile, sharing industry-related content, and engaging with others in your field. A strong personal brand can attract job offers, speaking engagements, and consulting opportunities.

8. Managing and Optimizing Earned Income

Effective management of earned income is essential for financial stability and growth. Here are strategies to help manage and optimize your income:

Budgeting and Saving

Creating a budget helps track expenses and identify savings opportunities. Setting financial goals can provide direction and motivation:

- **Track Expenses:** Monitor your spending to identify areas where you can cut costs. Use budgeting apps like Mint or YNAB to simplify the process.

- **Set Financial Goals:** Define clear financial goals, such as saving for a down payment on a house, building an emergency fund, or planning for retirement. Break these goals into smaller, achievable milestones.
- **Save Regularly:** Establish a habit of saving a portion of your income each month. Automate savings transfers to ensure consistency.

Investing Wisely

Investing earned income in stocks, real estate, or retirement accounts can grow your wealth over time. Diversifying investments reduces risk and enhances potential returns:

- **Stock Market:** Invest in a diversified portfolio of stocks, bonds, and mutual funds. Consider using robo-advisors or consulting with a financial advisor to create a balanced investment strategy.
- **Real Estate:** Real estate investments can provide rental income and potential appreciation. Research the local market and consider investing in properties that generate positive cash flow.
- **Retirement Accounts:** Contribute to retirement accounts like 401(k)s and IRAs. Take advantage of employer matching contributions and the tax benefits these accounts offer.

Tax Considerations

Understanding tax obligations and planning accordingly can optimize your earned income. Consulting with a tax professional can ensure compliance and identify potential deductions:

- **Tax Planning:** Estimate your annual tax liability and plan accordingly. Make quarterly estimated tax payments if you are self-employed or have additional income sources.
- **Deductions and Credits:** Identify potential tax deductions and credits that can reduce your taxable income. Common deductions include mortgage interest, student loan interest, and charitable contributions.
- **Professional Advice:** Consult with a tax professional or accountant to ensure you are taking advantage of all available tax benefits and remaining compliant with tax laws.

Conclusion

Earned income is a cornerstone of financial independence. By exploring various avenues, from traditional employment to side hustles, individuals can maximize their earning potential. Continuous learning, strategic planning, and effective management are key to leveraging earned income for long-term wealth. Diversifying income streams further enhances financial security and opens up new opportunities for growth.

In summary, the path to maximizing earned income involves:

- **Strategic Career Planning:** Pursue career advancement, continuing education, and skill development to increase your earning potential.
- **Networking and Personal Branding:** Build a strong professional network and personal brand to attract new opportunities.
- **Effective Income Management:** Budget effectively, save regularly, invest wisely, and plan for taxes to optimize your financial stability and growth.

By following these strategies, individuals can enhance their financial independence and create a more secure and prosperous future.

Chapter 4

Resale Profit

1. Introduction to Resale Profit

Resale profit is the income generated by purchasing items at a lower price and selling them at a higher price. This business model leverages the ability to identify undervalued goods and resell them for a profit, making it a potent strategy for wealth-building. The range of items that can be resold is vast, including vintage clothing, electronics, furniture, and collectibles. Understanding the nuances of different markets and the demand for specific products is essential for success in resale. The resale profit model is not only a primary source of income for many entrepreneurs but also a significant contributor to diversifying income streams and achieving financial independence. By effectively managing resale activities, individuals can create a reliable and scalable business model that contributes to long-term financial stability.

2. Types of Resale Businesses

There are various types of resale businesses, each with its unique opportunities and challenges:

Retail Arbitrage

Retail arbitrage is a strategy where individuals buy products from retail stores at discounted prices and then resell those same products online at higher prices to make a profit. This method is commonly used on popular e-commerce platforms like Amazon and eBay. The key idea behind retail arbitrage is to find and exploit price differences between the retail store and the online market for a particular product.

Step-By-Step Guide To Retail Arbitrage

Here's a step-by-step explanation of how retail arbitrage works:

Sourcing Products: Arbitrageurs (people who practice arbitrage) visit brick-and-mortar retail stores, such as big-box stores, department stores, or even local shops, to look for discounted items. They may target clearance sections, limited-time promotions, or store-specific discounts. The goal is to find products that are being sold at a lower price in the retail store compared to their online market value.

Price Discrepancy: The success of retail arbitrage relies on identifying a significant price discrepancy between the retail store and the online market for a particular product. For example, a book might be on clearance for $5 in a retail store but regularly sells for $20 online. Arbitrageurs use price scanners or comparison apps to quickly check online prices while they're in the store, helping them identify profitable opportunities.

Buying the Products: Once arbitrageurs find products with favorable price discrepancies, they purchase them from the retail store. They may buy a few units or bulk quantities, depending on the perceived demand and profit potential. It's important to note that some retailers may have policies against reselling, so arbitrageurs should be aware of any restrictions.

Listing and Selling Online: After purchasing the products, arbitrageurs list them for sale on online marketplaces like Amazon or eBay. They set the selling price higher than their purchase price but still competitive enough to attract buyers. The listing should include clear and attractive product descriptions, high-quality photos, and accurate information to increase the chances of a sale.

Shipping and Customer Service: When a product sells, the arbitrageur ships it to the buyer. They may use fulfillment services offered by platforms like Amazon (Fulfilled by Amazon) or handle shipping themselves. Providing good customer service is essential to maintain positive feedback and seller ratings, which can impact future sales.

Profits: The profit from retail arbitrage comes from the difference between the purchase price and the selling price, minus any associated fees and shipping costs. Arbitrageurs aim to maximize their profits by finding products with the largest price discrepancies and keeping their expenses low.

Retail arbitrage can be a lucrative business, but it also has its challenges and considerations:

Time and Effort: Arbitrageurs need to invest time in sourcing products, visiting stores, and managing online listings. It's not a passive income stream and requires consistent effort.

Competition: Retail arbitrage has become increasingly popular, leading to more competition. Arbitrageurs need to be quick in identifying deals and acting upon them before others do.

Inventory Management: Arbitrageurs must manage their inventory levels carefully to avoid being stuck with unsold products or running out of stock when demand is high.

Fees and Expenses: Online marketplaces charge listing fees, transaction fees, and sometimes additional fees for special services. Arbitrageurs need to factor in these costs when calculating their profits.

Customer Returns and Feedback: Handling customer returns, complaints, and negative feedback is part of the business. Providing good customer service is crucial for maintaining a positive seller reputation.

Overall, retail arbitrage can be a viable option for individuals looking to start an online business with relatively low upfront costs. However, success requires dedication, a good eye for deals, and a willingness to stay ahead of the competition.

Online Marketplaces

An online marketplace is a digital platform that connects buyers and sellers, allowing them to exchange goods and services over the internet. These marketplaces typically operate as intermediaries, providing a convenient and secure environment for transactions. Sellers can list their products or services on the platform, and buyers can browse and purchase items from multiple vendors in a single location.Online marketplaces, such as eBay, Etsy, and Facebook Marketplace, provide individuals with platforms to sell new and used items directly to consumers. These marketplaces have revolutionized the way people buy and sell goods, offering convenience, a wide reach, and a user-friendly interface.

Detailed Guide to Online Marketplaces

Here's a more detailed explanation of online marketplaces and how they work:

Broad Audience Reach: Online marketplaces attract a vast number of buyers and sellers from all over the world. This broad audience reach makes it easier for sellers to connect with potential customers without having to build their own e-commerce websites from scratch.

Convenience and Accessibility: These platforms offer a convenient and user-friendly interface for both buyers and sellers. Sellers can create listings from the comfort of their homes, providing detailed descriptions, photos, and even videos of their items. Buyers can easily search for specific products, compare prices, and make purchases with just a few clicks.

Variety of Items: Online marketplaces cater to a wide range of product categories. Popular items sold on these platforms include vintage clothing, handmade crafts, second-hand electronics, home decor, collectibles, books, and much more. Each platform may have its own specific niche or focus, so sellers should choose the most suitable platform for their products.

Listing Fees and Policies: Each online marketplace has its own set of fees, policies, and guidelines. For example, some platforms charge a listing fee for each item posted, while others take a percentage of the final sale price. Sellers should carefully review the terms and conditions, payment policies, and customer protection measures offered by each platform before deciding where to list their items.

Customer Service and Feedback: Providing excellent customer service is crucial for building a positive reputation on online marketplaces. Sellers are often rated and reviewed by buyers, and these ratings can impact their visibility and trustworthiness on the platform. Responding promptly to inquiries, offering refunds or exchanges when necessary, and maintaining good communication are essential aspects of successful selling.

Payment Processing: Online marketplaces typically offer integrated payment processing systems, making transactions secure and convenient for both buyers and sellers. These systems may include options like credit card payments, digital wallets, or platform-specific payment methods.

Marketing and Promotion: Sellers on online marketplaces can utilize various marketing tools provided by the platforms, such as promoted listings, targeted advertising, or social media integration, to increase the visibility of their items and attract more buyers.

Key Investments for Successful Sellers

To maximize profits and stand out in a competitive market, successful sellers often invest in the following:

High-Quality Product Photos: Clear, well-lit, and visually appealing photos are essential for attracting buyers. Professional-looking images can showcase the item from different angles and highlight its features and condition.

Detailed Descriptions: Accurate and detailed product descriptions help buyers make informed decisions. Sellers should include information such as dimensions, materials, condition, and any unique features or history of the item.

Customer Service: Prompt responses to inquiries, friendly communication, and accommodating return policies contribute to positive customer experiences and can lead to higher seller ratings and more sales.

Market Research: Understanding the market value of similar items and setting competitive prices can increase the likelihood of a sale. Sellers should also be aware of any seasonal trends or fluctuations in demand for their products.

Real Estate Flipping

Real estate flipping is a business strategy where investors buy properties, often at a discount or in a distressed state, make necessary improvements and renovations, and then sell them for a higher price to earn a profit. This type of resale requires a significant amount of capital to invest in properties and a solid understanding of the real estate market.

Strategies for Successful Real Estate Flipping

Identifying Profitable Properties: Successful real estate flippers have a keen eye for identifying properties with potential. This often involves targeting distressed or undervalued properties that can be acquired at a lower price. Distressed properties may include foreclosures, short sales, estate sales, or properties in need of significant repairs. Flippers also consider the location, market value, and potential for value appreciation when choosing properties.

Securing Financing: Real estate flipping typically requires a substantial financial investment. Flippers may use their own capital, obtain loans or mortgages, or partner with other investors to secure the necessary funds. It's important to carefully assess the potential profitability of a flip before committing to a purchase.

Making Improvements: Once a property is acquired, flippers focus on making strategic improvements and renovations to increase its value. This may involve cosmetic upgrades such as painting, landscaping, or modernizing fixtures and finishes. In some cases, more extensive renovations may be required, such as updating plumbing or electrical systems, remodeling kitchens or bathrooms, or adding additional living space.

Adding Value: The key to successful real estate flipping is adding value to the property. Flippers aim to make improvements that align with current market trends and buyer preferences. This may include opening up floor plans, creating additional living spaces, adding energy-efficient features, or incorporating smart home technology. Understanding the target market and making improvements that appeal to potential buyers is crucial.

Marketing and Staging: Effective marketing and staging strategies play a vital role in selling a flipped property. Flippers may hire professional photographers to capture high-quality images of the renovated property and create attractive listings. Staging the property with furniture and decor can help potential buyers visualize themselves living there and increase the perceived value of the home.

Selling for a Profit: The ultimate goal of real estate flipping is to sell the property at a higher price than the total investment (purchase price plus renovation costs). Flippers work with real estate agents or sell the property themselves, depending on their expertise and local regulations. Negotiation skills come into play during the selling process to maximize profits while still attracting buyers.

Managing Risks: Real estate flipping carries certain risks, such as unexpected renovation costs, changes in market conditions, or delays in finding buyers. Successful flippers carefully assess and mitigate these risks by conducting thorough due diligence, creating realistic budgets, and having contingency plans in place. Building a network of reliable contractors and professionals can also help manage risks and ensure timely and efficient renovations.

Real estate flipping can be a lucrative business, but it requires a deep understanding of the local real estate market, strong negotiation and renovation skills, and the ability to manage risks effectively. It may take time and experience to identify the most profitable properties and develop a successful flipping strategy.

Collectibles and Antiques

Collectibles: Collectibles refer to items that are sought after, bought, and sold primarily due to their perceived value or rarity. These items can be mass-produced or unique, and may include items like stamps, coins, sports cards, comic books, action figures, dolls, and more. The value of collectibles often increases over time due to factors such as limited supply, historical significance, or nostalgia. Collectors typically focus on acquiring and preserving items within a specific theme, era, or genre.

Antiques: Antiques are items that are at least 100 years old and have historical, artistic, or cultural significance. These items can include furniture, artwork, jewelry, textiles, ceramics, and other decorative or functional objects. Antiques are often valued for their craftsmanship, rarity, and provenance (the history of ownership), as well as their age. They can be found in various settings, such as antique shops, auctions, estate sales, and online marketplaces.

Reselling collectibles, antiques, and rare items can be a profitable venture if you have a good understanding of their market value and the demand within the collector community. This category of resale includes a wide range of items, such as coins, stamps, artwork, vintage toys, antique furniture, rare books, collectibles, and memorabilia.

Essential Strategies for Reselling Collectibles and Antiques

Market Knowledge: Success in reselling collectibles and antiques relies heavily on having extensive knowledge about the market and specific items. Collectors and resellers need to understand the factors that influence an item's value, such as rarity, condition, historical significance, and current market trends. Building expertise in a particular niche, such as vintage watches or antique porcelain, can give resellers an edge in identifying valuable items.

Sourcing Collectibles: Resellers of collectibles and antiques source their inventory through various channels. They may frequent estate sales, auctions, garage sales, thrift stores, or antique shops to find hidden gems. Building relationships with auctioneers, estate sale organizers, and other collectors can provide access to valuable items before they reach the general market.

Research and Authentication: Proper research and authentication are critical when dealing with collectibles and antiques. Resellers need to verify the authenticity, provenance, and condition of the items they acquire. This may involve studying reference books, consulting experts, or using online databases and price guides. Properly documenting the history and ownership of an item can also enhance its value and appeal to buyers.

Building a Collection: Some resellers focus on building a curated collection of related items, which can attract specialized buyers or collectors. For example, a reseller might assemble a collection of vintage comic books featuring a specific character or a set of antique silverware from a renowned manufacturer. Building a collection can increase the overall value and appeal to collectors seeking specific items to complete their sets.

Online Marketplaces: Online platforms, such as eBay, Etsy, or specialized collectible websites, provide a vast marketplace for reselling collectibles and antiques. These platforms offer access to a global audience of buyers and collectors. Creating detailed listings with high-quality photos, accurate descriptions, and transparent information about the item's condition and provenance is essential for attracting serious buyers.

Networking and Relationships: Building relationships with other collectors, dealers, and experts in the field can be advantageous. Networking can provide access to insider knowledge, rare items, and potential buyers. Attending collector conventions, joining clubs or associations, and participating in online forums can help resellers stay informed about market trends, upcoming auctions, and valuable finds.

Pricing and Negotiation: Pricing collectibles and antiques accurately is an art. Resellers need to strike a balance between maximizing profits and setting realistic prices that attract buyers. Understanding the demand for specific items, studying past sales data, and staying updated on market fluctuations are crucial for pricing items competitively. Negotiation skills also come into play, as collectors often expect some flexibility in pricing, especially for higher-value items.

Brick-and-Mortar Resale Shops

Brick-and-mortar resale shops refer to physical stores that specialize in selling second-hand or pre-owned goods. These stores cater to local markets and offer a unique in-person shopping experience for customers.

Types and Benefits of Brick-and-Mortar Resale Shops

Thrift Stores: Thrift stores, also known as charity shops or second-hand stores, are popular brick-and-mortar resale shops. They typically source their inventory through donations from individuals or organizations. Thrift stores often have a wide variety of items, including clothing, accessories, furniture, household goods, books, and decorative items. The prices in thrift stores are usually very affordable, attracting a diverse range of customers looking for bargains or unique finds. Many thrift stores are operated by charitable organizations, and the profits generated are used to support various community initiatives.

Antique Shops: Antique shops are another type of brick-and-mortar resale store that focuses specifically on selling antique or vintage items. These shops cater to collectors, enthusiasts, and individuals seeking unique, older pieces. Antique shops often have a more curated and specialized inventory, including furniture, artwork, jewelry, collectibles, and other items with historical or sentimental value. The owners or operators of antique shops typically have a strong knowledge of the items they sell, including their history, rarity, and market value.

Building a Loyal Customer Base: One of the advantages of brick-and-mortar resale shops is the ability to build a loyal customer base within the local community. Regular customers may visit the store frequently to browse new inventory, hunt for hidden treasures, or seek specific items. Developing relationships with customers and understanding their preferences can help shop owners cater to their clientele and create a personalized shopping experience.

Unique In-Person Shopping Experience: Brick-and-mortar resale shops offer a tactile and sensory shopping experience that cannot be replicated online. Customers can physically inspect the items, try on clothing, feel the fabric, or examine the craftsmanship of antique furniture. This hands-on experience, along with the thrill of discovering unique items, creates a sense of excitement and spontaneity that attracts many shoppers.

Store Atmosphere and Customer Service: The atmosphere and customer service in brick-and-mortar resale shops can also set them apart. Shop owners may create a welcoming and inviting ambiance, incorporating creative displays, background music, and friendly staff interactions. Providing excellent customer service, offering advice or assistance, and building relationships with customers can foster loyalty and repeat visits.

Community Engagement: Brick-and-mortar resale shops often become integral parts of their local communities. They may collaborate with local charities or organizations, host fundraising events, or participate in community initiatives. This engagement not only contributes to the shop's reputation but also strengthens its connection with the surrounding neighborhood and its residents.

Inventory Management and Sourcing: Owners of brick-and-mortar resale shops need to carefully manage their inventory to ensure a fresh selection of items for customers. They may source inventory through donations, estate sales, auctions, or direct purchases from individuals looking to sell their belongings. Constantly refreshing the inventory helps attract repeat customers and keeps the shopping experience exciting and unpredictable.

Flea Markets and Garage Sales

Flea markets and garage sales are popular venues for selling a wide variety of second-hand items, offering direct customer interactions and the potential for quick turnover of inventory.

Flea Markets: Flea markets are typically large outdoor markets where multiple vendors or individuals set up stalls or booths to sell their goods. These markets usually operate on specific days or weekends and attract a diverse range of buyers and sellers. Flea markets provide an opportunity for sellers to interact directly with customers, negotiate prices, and sell a wide array of items, including collectibles, antiques, vintage clothing, handmade crafts, used books, furniture, and miscellaneous household goods.

Garage Sales: Garage sales, also known as yard sales or rummage sales, are events where individuals or families sell their unwanted items directly from their homes. Garage sales are often held on weekends and may be advertised locally or through online platforms. They offer a convenient way for people to declutter their homes and make some extra money by selling items they no longer need. Garage sales usually have a more casual and intimate setting, allowing buyers to browse through a mix of used clothing, toys, furniture, appliances, and other miscellaneous items.

Quick Turnover and Direct Interactions: One of the advantages of selling at flea markets and garage sales is the potential for quick turnover of inventory. Sellers can offload a large number of items within a short period, making it ideal for those looking to declutter or generate immediate cash. Direct interactions with customers also allow sellers to negotiate prices, upsell complementary items, or build relationships that may lead to repeat business.

Customer Engagement and Bargaining: Flea markets and garage sales encourage face-to-face customer engagement and bargaining. Customers often expect to haggle over prices, and sellers can use their negotiation skills to close deals. This interactive aspect adds a layer of excitement and creates a sense of satisfaction for both buyers and sellers.

Low Overhead Costs: Setting up a stall at a flea market or hosting a garage sale typically involves low overhead costs compared to operating a brick-and-mortar store. Sellers at flea markets usually pay a small fee for their booth space, while garage sales have minimal expenses. This low-cost structure makes these venues accessible to individuals looking to make extra money without significant financial investment.

Community Building: Flea markets and garage sales often foster a sense of community and social interaction. They bring together people from diverse backgrounds, creating opportunities for social connections and local networking. Regular customers may become familiar faces, and sellers can establish relationships with fellow vendors, creating a supportive environment.

Unpredictable Inventory and Treasure Hunting: The inventory at flea markets and garage sales is often unpredictable, making the shopping experience a treasure hunt for buyers. Customers never know what unique or valuable items they might discover. This element of surprise and the possibility of finding hidden gems contribute to the excitement and appeal of these venues.

Consignment Shops

Consignment shops are retail businesses that sell second-hand items on behalf of the original owners. They act as intermediaries between the seller (consignor) and the buyer, taking a commission on each sale. Consignment shops offer a unique resale model that reduces risk for sellers while providing a steady stream of inventory for the shop.

How Consignment Shops Work

In a consignment shop, individuals bring their gently used or unwanted items to the store and agree to have them sold on consignment. The shop owner assesses the items, sets a selling price, and displays them in the store. When an item sells, the shop owner takes a predetermined percentage of the sale price as their commission, and the remaining amount is given to the original owner. This model allows individuals to sell their items without the hassle of managing their own sales or marketing.

Advantages of Consignment Shops

Reduced Risk for Sellers: Consignment shops provide a risk-reduced selling option for individuals who may not want to deal with the uncertainties of direct selling. The shop owner handles pricing, marketing, displaying, and selling the items, taking on the responsibility of finding buyers and completing transactions. This arrangement is particularly attractive to those who lack the time or expertise to sell their items independently.

Steady Stream of Inventory: Consignment shops benefit from a constant influx of new inventory, ensuring a diverse and ever-changing selection of items for customers. As items are sold, consignors bring in more goods, keeping the shop's offerings fresh and appealing. This steady stream of inventory helps attract repeat customers who enjoy the thrill of discovering different items with each visit.

Commission Structure: The commission rate varies among consignment shops and is typically agreed upon between the shop owner and the consignor before the items are accepted. The commission covers the shop's expenses, including rent, marketing, staffing, and other operational costs. Consignors benefit from the shop's expertise in pricing, merchandising, and attracting buyers, increasing the likelihood of a successful sale.

Authentication and Quality Control: Consignment shops often have processes in place to authenticate and evaluate the quality of the items they accept. This adds a layer of trust and confidence for buyers, who can be assured that the items they purchase are genuine and in good condition. Consignment shops may specialize in specific categories, such as designer clothing, vintage furniture, or luxury accessories, further enhancing their expertise and attracting a targeted customer base.

Marketing and Customer Reach: Consignment shops handle the marketing and promotion of the items they accept, leveraging their customer base and online presence to reach a wider audience. They may utilize social media, online marketplaces, or local advertising to showcase their inventory and attract potential buyers. This marketing support benefits consignors, as their items gain exposure to a larger pool of prospective purchasers.

Convenience and Customer Service: Consignment shops offer convenience to both sellers and buyers. Sellers can declutter their homes or refresh their wardrobes without the hassle of organizing their sales, while buyers can find unique, pre-owned items at often more affordable prices compared to buying new. Consignment shops also provide customer service, handling inquiries, returns, and exchanges, creating a positive shopping experience.

3. Finding Resale Opportunities

Market Research

Conducting thorough market research is the first step in finding profitable resale opportunities. This involves understanding demand, price trends, and consumer preferences to identify items that can be resold at a profit. Here are several methods and tools to assist in this process:

1. **Google Trends**: This tool allows you to see how frequently specific terms are being searched for on Google. By analyzing trends, you can gauge the

popularity of certain items and predict future demand.

2. **Market Reports**: Industry-specific market reports provide valuable insights into trends, growth areas, and consumer behavior. These reports can often be found through industry associations, market research firms, or financial news websites.

3. **Online Forums and Social Media**: Platforms like Reddit, Facebook groups, and other online communities can be goldmines for understanding consumer interests and discovering niche markets. Engaging with these communities can reveal what products are currently in demand.

4. **Competitive Analysis**: Investigate what other resellers are doing. Look at successful listings on platforms like eBay, Amazon, and Etsy to understand what types of items are selling well and at what prices.

Sourcing Products

Finding reliable sources for products is crucial for a successful resale business. Here are some potential sources:

1. **Wholesale Suppliers**: Establish connections with wholesalers who can provide products in bulk at

lower prices. Websites like Alibaba or local trade shows can be good starting points.

2. **Estate Sales**: Estate sales often feature a wide variety of items at discounted prices. Attending these sales can yield unique, high-value items.
3. **Thrift Stores**: Regular visits to thrift stores can uncover hidden gems. Look for items in good condition that are significantly underpriced.
4. **Auctions**: Online and live auctions can be excellent sources for acquiring valuable items at competitive prices. Websites like eBay, Bonhams, and local auction houses can provide opportunities to bid on various items.
5. **Building Relationships with Suppliers**: Developing strong relationships with suppliers can lead to access to high-quality products at lower prices. Trust and regular business can result in better deals and early access to new inventory.

Evaluating Potential Profitability

Before purchasing an item for resale, it's essential to evaluate its potential profitability. Consider the following factors:

1. **Purchase Price**: Ensure that the initial cost of the item is low enough to allow for a profitable resale.
2. **Shipping Costs**: Account for the cost of shipping when evaluating an item's profitability. Heavy or bulky items may incur higher shipping costs.
3. **Fees**: Consider any platform fees, payment processing fees, or taxes that will be deducted from your selling price.
4. **Expected Selling Price**: Research what similar items have sold for recently. Platforms like eBay offer a "sold items" search filter that can provide historical sales data.
5. **Profit Calculators**: Use online profit calculators to input your costs and potential selling price to determine if the profit margin meets your expectations.

4. Valuing and Pricing Items

Valuing Items: Valuing an item refers to the process of determining its worth or significance based on various factors. This process often involves researching and considering the item's historical background, rarity, condition, provenance, demand, and comparable sales data. Valuations can be performed by professional appraisers, auction houses, or through personal research using available resources. While Pricing Items: Pricing items involves setting a specific monetary value or asking price for the item, based on its valuation. This process considers various factors, such as the target market, competition, profit margins, and overall business strategy. Correctly valuing and pricing items ensures competitive-ness and profitability.

Here's how to approach this:

Assessing Item Value

1. **Research Similar Items**: Look up similar items on various resale platforms to understand their current market value. Pay attention to factors like brand, condition, age, and demand.
2. **Condition**: Items in mint or excellent condition will typically fetch higher prices than those with wear and tear. Be honest about the condition of your items to maintain buyer trust.
3. **Brand and Rarity**: Well-known brands and rare items often command higher prices. Limited edition or discontinued items can be particularly valuable.

Pricing Strategies

Pricing strategies are the methods and approaches businesses use to determine the prices of their products or services. These strategies aim to balance profitability, competitiveness, and customer demand while considering various factors such as production costs, market conditions, and the company's overall objectives. Some common pricing strategies include:

1. Cost-plus Pricing: This strategy involves adding a fixed percentage markup to the production or acquisition cost of an item to determine its selling price. It is a straightforward approach that ensures a predetermined profit margin but may not consider market demand or competitor pricing.

2. Competition-based Pricing: In this strategy, businesses set their prices based on the prices of their competitors. Companies may choose to price their products below, at, or above the competition, depending on factors like market share, product differentiation, and target audience.

3. Value-based Pricing: This strategy involves setting prices based on the perceived value of a product or service to the customer rather than its production cost or competitor pricing. Companies using this strategy aim to position their products as high-quality, premium offerings and charge accordingly.

4. Penetration Pricing: A strategy used to enter a new market or gain market share, penetration pricing involves setting low prices initially to attract customers and drive sales. Once the company has established a

customer base, it may raise prices to increase profitability.

5. Price Skimming: This strategy involves setting high initial prices for a new product to maximize profits from early adopters or customers willing to pay a premium. Over time, as competition increases or the product becomes more widely adopted, the company may lower prices to maintain sales volume.

6. Dynamic Pricing: Also known as surge pricing or time-based pricing, this strategy involves adjusting prices based on real-time market conditions, such as demand, supply, and competitor activity. Dynamic pricing is often used in industries like hospitality, transportation, and e-commerce.

7. Bundle Pricing: This strategy involves selling multiple products or services together as a package at a discounted price. Bundle pricing can increase sales, encourage customers to try new products, and clear inventory.

8. Psychological Pricing: This strategy involves setting prices that exploit cognitive biases or consumer psychology to influence buying decisions. Examples include using charm pricing (e.g., pricing at $9.99 instead of $10) or offering buy-one-get-one-free deals.

9. **Competitive Pricing**: To attract buyers, set your prices competitively compared to similar items. This doesn't necessarily mean the lowest price but rather a price that offers good value while ensuring profitability.
10. **Bulk Purchase Discounts**: Offer discounts for bulk purchases to encourage larger orders and move more inventory quickly.
11. **Loyalty Discounts**: Consider offering discounts to repeat customers to build loyalty and encourage future purchases.

Market Considerations

1. **Platform-Specific Pricing**: Adjust your pricing based on the platform you are using. Some platforms, like Etsy, may support higher prices for handmade or vintage items, while others, like eBay, may be more price-sensitive.
2. **Target Audience**: Understand your target audience's willingness to pay. Higher prices may be justified for unique or high-demand items that cater to a niche market.
3. **Seasonal Adjustments**: Adjust your pricing based on seasonal demand. For example, certain toys may sell for higher prices during the holiday season,

while summer sports equipment may fetch better prices in spring or early summer.

Conclusion

Finding resale opportunities involves diligent market research, strategic sourcing, and careful evaluation of potential profitability. By understanding how to value and price items correctly, you can ensure competitiveness and profitability in your resale business. Adopting these strategies will help you identify profitable opportunities and build a successful resale enterprise.

5. Selling Platforms and Strategies

Choosing the right platform and strategy is essential to maximizing resale profit. Different platforms cater to different types of products and customer bases, and each has its own set of advantages and considerations. Here are some key platforms and strategies to consider:

Online Platforms

1. **eBay**
    - **Advantages**: Wide reach, auction-style and fixed-price listings, extensive categories.
    - **Considerations**: Listing fees, final value fees, shipping costs, and competitive marketplace.

- **Strategy**: Utilize eBay's global reach to sell a diverse range of items. Optimize listings with high-quality photos, detailed descriptions, and competitive pricing. Consider using eBay's auction format for rare or high-demand items to potentially drive up the selling price.

2. **Amazon**
    - **Advantages**: Huge customer base, fulfillment services (FBA), trusted platform.
    - **Considerations**: Selling fees, strict policies, and high competition.
    - **Strategy**: Focus on popular, high-demand products that fit well within Amazon's ecosystem. Use Fulfillment by Amazon (FBA) to take advantage of Amazon's logistics and customer service, making the buying process smoother for customers.

3. **Etsy**
    - **Advantages**: Specialized in handmade, vintage, and unique items, niche market.
    - **Considerations**: Listing fees, commission fees, and a more niche audience.
    - **Strategy**: Leverage Etsy's focus on handmade and vintage items to sell unique products. Build a strong brand presence with well-designed

storefronts, compelling product stories, and excellent customer service.

Social Media and Personal Websites

1. **Social Media Platforms**
    - **Instagram and Facebook**: These platforms are excellent for marketing items and building a brand presence.
    - **Strategy**: Use visually appealing posts, stories, and ads to showcase products. Engage with followers through comments, messages, and interactive content. Utilize Facebook Marketplace for direct sales and Instagram's shopping features for seamless purchasing experiences.

2. **Personal Website**
    - **Advantages**: Complete control over the sales process, no platform fees, brand building.
    - **Strategy**: Create a professional, easy-to-navigate website to showcase and sell products. Use SEO techniques to drive organic traffic and consider integrating a blog to provide valuable content related to your products. Offer exclusive deals and promotions to encourage direct purchases.

Offline Selling Strategies
1. **Local Flea Markets and Craft Fairs**
    - **Advantages**: Direct customer interaction, no shipping costs, cash sales.
    - **Strategy**: Participate in local markets and fairs to build a local customer base. Display items attractively, offer special deals, and engage with customers to build relationships. Collect contact information to keep in touch with customers about future events and new products.
2. **Community Events**
    - **Advantages**: Networking opportunities, community support, word-of-mouth marketing.
    - **Strategy**: Get involved in community events and fairs to increase visibility. Offer demonstrations or workshops to showcase your products and expertise. Building relationships with local customers can lead to repeat business and referrals.

6. Strategies for Maximizing Resale Profit

Effective marketing and branding, along with strategic pricing and negotiation, can significantly boost resale profit.

Building a Brand

1. **Create a Recognizable Brand**
    - **Strategy**: Develop a brand that reflects the values and unique selling points of your business. Use consistent branding across all platforms, including logos, color schemes, and messaging. A strong brand helps build trust and customer loyalty.

Effective Marketing Techniques

1. **Social Media Marketing**
    - **Strategy**: Leverage social media platforms to reach a wider audience. Use high-quality photos and videos to showcase products, run targeted ads, and engage with followers through posts, stories, and live sessions.
2. **Email Campaigns**
    - **Strategy**: Build an email list to keep customers informed about new products, promotions, and sales. Use personalized emails to engage with customers and encourage repeat purchases.
3. **Search Engine Optimization (SEO)**
    - **Strategy**: Optimize your website and product listings with relevant keywords to improve search engine rankings. High-quality content,

backlinks, and regular updates can help drive organic traffic to your site.

4. **High-Quality Photos and Descriptions**
    - **Strategy**: Use professional-quality photos and detailed, accurate descriptions to enhance product listings. Highlight key features, benefits, and any unique selling points to attract potential buyers.

Customer Engagement and Retention

1. **Provide Excellent Customer Service**
    - **Strategy**: Respond promptly to inquiries, handle issues efficiently, and ensure a positive buying experience. Happy customers are more likely to become repeat buyers and recommend your business to others.
2. **Engage with Customers Through Social Media**
    - **Strategy**: Use social media to interact with customers, answer questions, and gather feedback. Engaging content and regular updates keep your audience interested and involved.
3. **Offer Loyalty Programs**
    - **Strategy**: Reward repeat customers with discounts, special offers, and exclusive access to new products. Loyalty programs can increase customer retention and lifetime value.

Pricing Strategies
1. **Research the Market**
    - **Strategy**: Conduct thorough market research to determine competitive pricing. Consider factors such as demand, condition, and rarity when pricing your items.
2. **Offer Bundle Deals**
    - **Strategy**: Encourage larger purchases by offering discounts on bundles or multiple items. This can increase your average order value and help move inventory more quickly.

Negotiation Techniques
1. **Negotiate Purchase Prices**
    - **Strategy**: When sourcing products, negotiate with suppliers to get the best possible prices. Building strong relationships can lead to better deals and exclusive offers.
2. **Be Open to Offers**
    - **Strategy**: When selling, be willing to consider reasonable offers but know your bottom line. Use negotiation skills to find a middle ground that satisfies both you and the buyer.
3. **Build Rapport with Buyers**
    - **Strategy**: Establish trust and rapport with customers through good communication and

service. Satisfied customers are more likely to return and recommend your business.

7. Operational Considerations

Efficient operations are essential for a successful resale business. Streamlined processes and effective management systems ensure that the business runs smoothly, reduces costs, and increases profitability. Here are some key operational considerations:

Inventory Management

1. **Track Inventory Levels**
   - **Strategy**: Regularly monitor your inventory to ensure you have enough stock to meet demand without overstocking. Use spreadsheets or inventory management software to track items, quantities, and locations.

2. **Analyze Sales Trends**
   - **Strategy**: Review past sales data to identify trends and adjust inventory accordingly. Understand which items are best-sellers and which are slow-moving to make informed purchasing decisions.

3. **Inventory Management Software**
   - **Strategy**: Implement inventory management software to automate tracking, reduce errors, and

streamline processes. Software solutions like TradeGecko, Zoho Inventory, or even simple tools like Excel can help manage inventory efficiently.

Shipping and Logistics
1. **Choose Reliable Shipping Methods**
    - **Strategy**: Partner with reputable shipping carriers to ensure timely and secure delivery of products. Offer multiple shipping options, including standard and expedited services, to meet different customer needs.
2. **Offer Tracking Options**
    - **Strategy**: Provide customers with tracking information to enhance transparency and build trust. This reduces customer inquiries about order status and improves the overall buying experience.
3. **Consider Packaging Costs**
    - **Strategy**: Factor in packaging costs when setting product prices. Use cost-effective, yet protective packaging materials to minimize expenses while ensuring items arrive undamaged.

4. **Optimize Delivery Times**
    - **Strategy**: Set realistic delivery times and communicate them clearly to customers. Efficient logistics planning can help meet or exceed delivery expectations, leading to higher customer satisfaction.

Financial Tracking and Reporting
1. **Maintain Accurate Records**
    - **Strategy**: Keep detailed records of all expenses, sales, and profits. This includes purchase receipts, shipping costs, platform fees, and other operating expenses.
2. **Use Accounting Software**
    - **Strategy**: Implement accounting software like QuickBooks, Xero, or FreshBooks to automate financial tracking and reporting. These tools can help monitor cash flow, manage invoices, and prepare for tax filings.
3. **Monitor Financial Performance**
    - **Strategy**: Regularly review financial reports to assess the health of your business. Track key metrics such as gross profit margin, net profit margin, and return on investment to make informed decisions and plan for growth.

4. **Plan for Growth**
    - **Strategy**: Use financial data to identify opportunities for expansion and investment. Create a budget and financial plan that outlines projected income, expenses, and growth strategies.

8. Case Studies

Examining successful resale businesses can provide valuable insights into effective strategies and best practices. Here are two case studies that highlight different approaches to resale:

Case Study: Vintage Clothing Store

Jane's Vintage Clothing Store on Etsy
- **Background**: Jane started her vintage clothing store by sourcing unique items from thrift stores and estate sales. She had a keen eye for fashion and a passion for vintage clothing.
- **Strategies**:
    - **Niche Market Focus**: Jane focused on building a niche market by offering carefully curated vintage clothing items. This helped her stand out in a crowded marketplace.

- **Attention to Detail**: She paid great attention to detail in product presentation. High-quality photos, detailed descriptions, and accurate measurements helped attract customers.
- **Customer Service**: Jane prioritized excellent customer service, responding promptly to inquiries and addressing any issues quickly. This led to positive reviews and repeat business.

- **Results**: Jane's meticulous approach and dedication to quality and customer service led to a loyal customer base and consistent sales growth. Her store became a go-to destination for vintage clothing enthusiasts.

Case Study: Electronics Reseller

John's Refurbished Electronics Business on eBay
- **Background**: John identified a demand for refurbished electronics on eBay. He started by purchasing items in bulk from liquidation sales and investing in repairs.
- **Strategies**:
  - **Bulk Purchasing**: John sourced electronics in bulk from liquidation sales, which allowed him to acquire products at a low cost.
  - **Refurbishment and Quality Assurance**: He invested in refurbishing the electronics and

implemented thorough testing and quality assurance processes. This ensured that the products he sold were reliable and met customer expectations.
- ○ **Competitive Pricing**: By keeping costs low and ensuring high quality, John was able to offer competitive prices that attracted buyers.
- **Results**: John's business model proved profitable as he built a reputation for selling high-quality refurbished electronics. His thorough testing and quality assurance processes led to high customer satisfaction and repeat business.

Conclusion

Efficient operations, strategic sourcing, and attention to customer needs are essential for a successful resale business. By implementing effective inventory management, reliable shipping and logistics, and accurate financial tracking, resellers can optimize their operations and maximize profitability. Learning from successful case studies provides valuable insights and inspiration for building a thriving resale business.

9. Challenges and Solutions

Resale businesses encounter various challenges that can impede growth and profitability. However, strategic solutions can effectively mitigate these obstacles. Here are some common challenges and their corresponding solutions:

Challenge: Competition

High competition in popular niches can drive prices down and make it difficult to stand out.

Solution: Differentiate Your Business

- **Unique Products**: Offer unique or hard-to-find items that are not readily available from other sellers. This can attract customers looking for something specific or rare.
- **Superior Customer Service**: Provide exceptional customer service by responding promptly to inquiries, resolving issues quickly, and offering a pleasant buying experience. Positive reviews and word-of-mouth referrals can set you apart from competitors.
- **Effective Branding**: Build a strong brand that resonates with your target audience. Develop a cohesive brand identity with consistent messaging, visuals, and values. A well-defined brand can create loyalty and recognition in a crowded market.

Challenge: Inventory Management

Managing inventory levels to avoid overstock or stockouts can be complex and challenging.

Solution: Use Inventory Management Tools and Data Analysis

- **Inventory Management Software**: Implement inventory management software to automate tracking and provide real-time data on stock levels. Tools like

TradeGecko, Zoho Inventory, or Excel can help streamline this process.
- **Demand Forecasting**: Use historical sales data and market trends to predict demand accurately. This helps optimize stock levels, ensuring you have enough inventory to meet customer needs without overstocking.
- **Regular Audits**: Conduct regular inventory audits to verify stock levels and identify discrepancies. This helps maintain accuracy and reduces the risk of stockouts or overstock.

Challenge: Shipping Costs

High shipping costs can significantly reduce profit margins, especially for bulky or heavy items.

Solution: Negotiate Bulk Shipping Rates and Optimize Packaging
- **Bulk Shipping Rates**: Negotiate with carriers for bulk shipping rates to reduce costs. Establishing relationships with shipping providers can lead to better rates and terms.
- **Optimize Packaging**: Use cost-effective, lightweight packaging materials to reduce shipping weight and size. Ensure that packaging is protective enough to prevent damage but not excessively heavy or bulky.
- **Shipping Options**: Offer multiple shipping options to customers, including standard, expedited, and economy

shipping. This allows customers to choose based on their budget and urgency, potentially sharing the cost burden.

Conclusion

Resale profit represents a versatile and accessible way to build wealth. By exploring various resale business models, finding and valuing profitable products, and leveraging effective selling and marketing strategies, individuals can maximize their resale profit potential. Continuous learning, strategic planning, and efficient operations are key to long-term success in the resale market. Overcoming challenges such as competition, inventory management, and shipping costs requires innovative solutions and a proactive approach.

By differentiating your business through unique offerings, superior customer service, and effective branding, you can stand out in a competitive market. Implementing inventory management tools and data analysis helps maintain optimal stock levels, while negotiating bulk shipping rates and optimizing packaging can reduce costs and enhance profitability.

The resale market offers significant opportunities for those willing to invest the time and effort to navigate its challenges. With a focus on continuous improvement and strategic execution, resale businesses can become a significant and sustainable income stream, contributing to long-term financial success.

Chapter 5

Rental Property

1. Introduction to Rental Property

Welcome to the fascinating world of rental property investing, a journey that promises not just financial rewards but also the potential for long-term wealth creation. In this introductory lecture, we will delve into the fundamentals of rental property income and why it is an essential concept in the realm of investment strategies.

Rental property income, at its core, involves leasing or renting out a real estate property to tenants in exchange for regular monthly rent payments. This income stream is more than just a source of cash flow; it is a cornerstone of building and growing wealth. The beauty of rental property income lies in its multi-faceted nature, offering not just immediate monetary benefits but also long-term gains.

Firstly, rental income provides a steady and consistent cash flow. By leasing your property to tenants, you generate a reliable income stream that can help cover expenses, pay down mortgages, or fund other investments. This passive income can be particularly attractive for those seeking financial freedom or looking to supplement their primary source of income.

But rental property investing goes beyond just the immediate cash flow. Over time, real estate properties tend to appreciate in value. This means that while you are collecting rent, your property's value is likely increasing. This property value appreciation can lead to significant capital gains when it comes time to sell, providing a substantial boost to your overall wealth.

Moreover, rental property ownership offers tax advantages that can further enhance your financial position. For instance, you may be able to deduct certain expenses related to the property, such as mortgage interest, property taxes, and maintenance costs, thereby reducing your taxable income. Additionally, depreciation, a non-cash expense, allows you to recover the cost of the property over time, resulting in further tax benefits.

Diversification is another key advantage of investing in rental properties. By adding real estate to your investment portfolio, you reduce your reliance on more traditional assets like stocks and bonds. This diversification can help mitigate risks, as the real estate market often moves independently of other markets, providing a hedge against economic fluctuations.

The rental property market has a proven track record of resilience and stability. Historically, it has weathered economic storms and often outperforms other investment vehicles in terms of returns. This stability is rooted in the fundamental need for shelter, ensuring a constant demand for rental properties.

2. Types of Rental Properties

Residential Properties
1. **Single-family Homes**
    - **Definition**: Standalone houses designed for a single family.
    - **Investor Appeal**: These properties are popular among investors due to their broad market appeal and relatively lower complexity in management. They attract a wide range of tenants, including families, young professionals, and retirees.
    - **Management**: Single-family homes typically require less intensive management compared to multi-family properties, as there are fewer tenants and maintenance issues to address.

2. **Multi-family Homes**
    - **Definition**: Properties that contain multiple separate living units, such as duplexes (two units), triplexes (three units), and apartment buildings (four or more units).
    - **Income Potential**: Multi-family homes offer higher income potential due to the multiple streams of rental income from each unit.
    - **Management**: These properties require more management and maintenance than single-family homes. Investors might need to deal with multiple tenants, coordinate repairs and maintenance for common areas, and possibly hire property management services.
3. **Condominiums and Apartments**
    - **Definition**: Units that are part of larger buildings. Condominiums (condos) can be individually owned, while apartments are typically rented out.
    - **Costs and Fees**: Condos often come with homeowner association (HOA) fees, which cover maintenance of common areas, amenities, and building services. Apartments

might involve dealing with management companies that handle leasing and maintenance.
- **Market Dynamics**: These properties can attract a diverse tenant base, including singles, couples, and small families. The appeal often depends on the location, amenities, and building quality.

Commercial Properties

1. **Office Spaces**
    - **Definition**: Buildings or portions of buildings rented to businesses for office use.
    - **Demand Drivers**: Economic growth and business expansions can drive the demand for office spaces. Companies looking to establish or expand their operations seek suitable office locations.
    - **Lease Terms**: Office leases are typically longer than residential leases, often ranging from 3 to 10 years. This can provide stable income for investors.

2. **Retail Spaces**
    - **Definition**: Properties leased to retail businesses, such as shops, restaurants, and service providers.
    - **Key Factors**: The success of retail properties heavily depends on location and foot traffic. High-visibility areas with significant pedestrian flow are highly desirable.
    - **Tenant Mix**: A diverse tenant mix can attract more customers to the location, enhancing the overall appeal of the retail property.
3. **Industrial Properties**
    - **Definition**: Properties that include warehouses, manufacturing plants, and distribution centers.
    - **Lease Characteristics**: Industrial properties often have longer lease terms, ranging from 5 to 20 years, and typically attract stable tenants.
    - **Specialized Management**: These properties may require specialized management due to

their unique needs, such as loading docks, storage space, and manufacturing facilities.

Vacation Rentals
1. **Short-term Rentals**
    - **Definition**: Properties rented out for short durations, often through platforms like Airbnb or Vrbo.
    - **Income Potential**: These rentals can generate higher per-night income compared to long-term leases but require constant management and marketing to maintain occupancy rates.
    - **Management Needs**: Short-term rentals demand frequent cleaning, guest communication, and maintenance to ensure a high-quality experience for guests.
2. **Seasonal Properties**
    - **Definition**: Properties located in vacation destinations that are rented out during peak seasons, such as summer beach houses or winter ski cabins.
    - **Income Dynamics**: These properties offer high income potential during peak seasons

but can remain vacant during off-seasons. Effective marketing and pricing strategies are essential to maximize occupancy and revenue.
- o **Management Considerations**: Managing seasonal properties involves preparing for high turnover rates during peak periods and ensuring the property is well-maintained during off-seasons to attract future guests.

3. Steps to Investing in Rental Properties

1. Market Research
- **Understanding Local Real Estate Trends**
  - o **Analyzing Local Market Conditions**: To make informed investment decisions, it is crucial to analyze local real estate market conditions. This involves examining property values, rental rates, and occupancy rates. You can use real estate websites like Zillow and Realtor.com, consult local market reports, and review economic data to gather valuable insights.

- **Examining Historical Trends**: Study the historical data of the market to understand how property values and rental rates have changed over time. This can help predict future trends and identify whether the market is appreciating or declining.
- **Identifying Growth Areas**: Look for areas that are experiencing economic growth, infrastructural development, and increasing population. These factors can contribute to higher property values and rental demand.

- **Analyzing Supply and Demand**
  - **Supply and Demand Dynamics**: Determine the balance between the number of available rental properties and the demand from tenants. In markets where demand is high and supply is low, rental rates are likely to be higher, and vacancy rates lower, making it a favorable investment environment.
  - **Vacancy Rates**: Low vacancy rates indicate strong rental demand and a higher likelihood of consistent rental income. High vacancy rates may suggest an oversaturated market or declining demand.

- **Rental Rate Comparisons**: Compare rental rates in different neighborhoods to identify areas where you can achieve higher returns on investment. Understanding the competition and setting competitive rental prices is essential for attracting tenants.

2. Financial Planning
- **Budgeting for Purchase and Maintenance**
  - **Comprehensive Budgeting**: Create a detailed budget that includes all costs associated with purchasing and maintaining a rental property. This should cover the purchase price, closing costs, renovation expenses, and ongoing maintenance costs. It's crucial to include a buffer for unexpected expenses to avoid financial strain.
  - **Cost Estimation Tools**: Use online calculators and tools to estimate renovation and maintenance costs. Consulting with contractors or property managers can also provide accurate cost projections.
  - **Cash Flow Analysis**: Calculate the expected rental income and compare it with your

expenses to determine the property's cash flow. Positive cash flow indicates that your rental income exceeds your expenses, making the investment financially viable.

- **Financing Options and Mortgage Considerations**
    - **Exploring Financing Options**: Investigate different financing options, including conventional mortgages, Federal Housing Administration (FHA) loans, and investment property loans. Each option has its own terms, interest rates, and requirements.
    - **Comparing Interest Rates and Terms**: Compare interest rates and loan terms from multiple lenders to find the most favorable financing option. Consider factors such as down payment requirements, loan duration, and prepayment penalties.
    - **Pre-Approval Process**: Obtain pre-approval for a mortgage to understand how much you can borrow and to streamline the purchasing process. Pre-approval demonstrates to sellers that you are a serious buyer with secure financing.

3. Property Selection
- **Identifying Profitable Locations**
    - **Neighborhood Analysis**: Focus on neighborhoods with strong rental demand, good schools, low crime rates, and amenities such as public transportation, shopping centers, and parks. These factors contribute to the desirability of the location and can attract quality tenants.
    - **Economic Indicators**: Look for areas with job growth and a stable economy. Locations with diverse employment opportunities tend to have a steady influx of potential tenants.
    - **Future Development Plans**: Research any planned infrastructure or commercial developments in the area. Upcoming projects like new roads, public facilities, or business centers can enhance the value and appeal of the property.
- **Evaluating Property Condition and Potential**
    - **Thorough Inspections**: Conduct comprehensive inspections to assess the property's condition. This includes evaluating the structural integrity, electrical

systems, plumbing, roofing, and overall maintenance. Identifying necessary repairs or upgrades beforehand can help you negotiate the purchase price and plan for renovations.

- **Professional Assessments**: Hire professional inspectors to identify any hidden issues that might not be apparent during a casual inspection. Their expertise can save you from unexpected repair costs in the future.
- **Layout and Size Considerations**: Consider the property's layout, size, and potential for rent increases. Properties with flexible layouts and adequate living space tend to attract a broader range of tenants and can command higher rental rates.
- **Investment Potential**: Evaluate the property's potential for appreciation and rental income growth. Properties in areas with increasing demand and limited supply are more likely to appreciate in value and provide higher returns on investment over time.

4. Managing Rental Properties

1. Tenant Acquisition
- **Marketing Rental Properties**
    - **Online Listings**: Utilize popular real estate websites like Zillow, Realtor.com, and Craigslist to list your rental properties. Include high-quality photos and detailed descriptions to attract potential tenants. Highlight key features such as location, amenities, and recent upgrades.
    - **Social Media**: Leverage social media platforms like Facebook, Instagram, and Twitter to reach a broader audience. Share posts in local community groups and real estate forums to increase visibility.
    - **Local Advertising**: Consider placing ads in local newspapers, community bulletin boards, and real estate magazines. Hosting open houses or property tours can also attract interested tenants.
    - **Real Estate Agents**: Partner with real estate agents who specialize in rental properties. They can provide valuable market insights,

access to potential tenants, and professional marketing services.

- **Screening and Selecting Tenants**
    - **Background Checks**: Conduct thorough background checks to verify the identity and history of potential tenants. This includes checking for criminal records, past evictions, and verifying references.
    - **Credit Checks**: Assess the creditworthiness of applicants by reviewing their credit reports. This helps determine their financial stability and ability to pay rent on time.
    - **Employment Verification**: Confirm the employment status and income of applicants to ensure they can afford the rent. Request recent pay stubs or an employment verification letter.
    - **Rental History**: Contact previous landlords to inquire about the applicant's rental history, including payment habits, property upkeep, and any issues that arose during their tenancy.

2. Lease Agreements

- **Crafting Effective Lease Contracts**
    - **Clear Terms**: Include detailed terms on rent amount, due dates, late fees, and acceptable payment methods. Clearly outline the security deposit amount, conditions for its return, and any deductions.
    - **Maintenance Responsibilities**: Specify the responsibilities of both the landlord and tenant regarding property maintenance and repairs. Clarify who handles lawn care, snow removal, and routine upkeep.
    - **Lease Duration**: Define the lease term (e.g., 12 months) and any conditions for renewal or termination. Include provisions for early termination, subletting, and lease modification.
    - **Compliance with Laws**: Ensure the lease complies with local landlord-tenant laws and regulations. Include clauses that address fair housing laws, tenant rights, and legal eviction procedures.
- **Understanding Legal Obligations**
    - **Landlord-Tenant Laws**: Familiarize

- yourself with local, state, and federal laws governing rental properties. This includes understanding tenant rights, security deposit regulations, and notice requirements for entering the property.
- **Fair Housing Regulations**: Adhere to fair housing laws that prohibit discrimination based on race, color, national origin, religion, sex, familial status, and disability. Ensure all marketing, tenant screening, and leasing practices are compliant.
- **Lease Termination Procedures**: Understand the legal procedures for terminating a lease, whether due to non-payment, lease violations, or tenant requests. Follow the proper steps for serving eviction notices and pursuing legal action if necessary.

3. Maintenance and Upkeep

- **Regular Maintenance Schedules**
  - **Preventive Maintenance**: Implement regular maintenance schedules to keep the property in good condition and prevent

major repairs. This includes HVAC servicing, plumbing checks, pest control, and roof inspections.
- **Seasonal Maintenance**: Conduct seasonal maintenance tasks such as gutter cleaning, furnace checks, and winterizing the property. Prepare the property for extreme weather conditions to avoid damage.
- **Tenant Responsibilities**: Clearly communicate the tenant's responsibilities for routine maintenance tasks, such as changing light bulbs, replacing air filters, and maintaining the cleanliness of the property.

- **Handling Repairs and Emergencies**
  - **Reporting System**: Establish a system for tenants to report maintenance issues and emergencies. This can be through a dedicated phone line, email, or online portal. Respond promptly to repair requests to maintain tenant satisfaction.
  - **Trusted Contractors**: Maintain a list of reliable and trusted contractors for various types of repairs, including plumbing, electrical work, and general maintenance.

Building good relationships with contractors can expedite repairs and ensure quality work.

- ○ **Emergency Preparedness**: Have a plan in place for handling emergencies such as water leaks, power outages, or natural disasters. Ensure tenants know how to contact you in case of an emergency and provide them with instructions for common emergency situations.

By meticulously managing tenant acquisition, lease agreements, and property maintenance, landlords can ensure their rental properties operate smoothly and remain profitable. Effective management practices lead to satisfied tenants, lower vacancy rates, and increased property value over time.

5. Maximizing Rental Income

1. **Setting Competitive Rent Prices**
   - Comparing Market Rates
     - ○ **Researching Comparable Properties**: Conduct thorough research on rental prices

for similar properties in your area. This involves looking at listings on real estate websites, consulting local rental market reports, and possibly engaging with real estate agents who have expertise in the local market.
- **Adjusting for Features and Location**: Compare your property's features—such as size, number of bedrooms and bathrooms, amenities, and overall condition—with those of nearby rentals. Consider the property's location, proximity to schools, public transportation, shopping centers, and other amenities when setting the rent price.
- **Monitoring Trends**: Stay updated on rental market trends to adjust your prices accordingly. Factors like seasonal demand, economic conditions, and changes in the neighborhood can affect rental prices.

- **Adjusting Rent Based on Property Value and Demand**
    - **Periodic Reviews**: Regularly review your rental prices to ensure they remain competitive and reflective of current market

conditions. Consider increases in property value due to renovations, neighborhood development, or general market appreciation.

- **Inflation and Market Changes**: Adjust rent to account for inflation and changes in the rental market. If demand for rentals in your area increases or if you've made significant improvements to the property, you can justify a higher rent.
- **Value-Based Adjustments**: Ensure the rent reflects the value provided to tenants. Properties with high-quality features, modern amenities, and excellent maintenance can command higher rents.

2. Value-Adding Renovations
- **Enhancing Property Appeal and Functionality**
    - **Modern Kitchens**: Upgrading kitchens with modern appliances, new countertops, cabinets, and flooring can significantly increase the property's appeal and rental value.

- **Updated Bathrooms**: Renovating bathrooms with new fixtures, tiles, and efficient plumbing can make the property more attractive to potential tenants.
- **Energy-Efficient Features**: Installing energy-efficient windows, insulation, and appliances can reduce utility costs for tenants and make the property more appealing. Features like solar panels can also add value.
- **Curb Appeal**: Improving the exterior appearance of the property with landscaping, painting, and repairing any visible damage can attract more tenants and justify higher rent.

- **Cost-Benefit Analysis of Renovations**
  - **Evaluating Potential Increases**: Before undertaking any renovation, calculate the potential increase in rental income. Determine if the increased rent will cover the renovation costs within a reasonable period.
  - **Prioritizing Renovations**: Focus on renovations that offer the highest return on

investment. Kitchen and bathroom upgrades, followed by energy-efficient improvements, typically provide the best returns.
- **Budgeting and Planning**: Develop a detailed budget and plan for renovations. Ensure the improvements align with market demand and tenant preferences in your area.

3. Reducing Vacancy Rates
- **Effective Tenant Retention Strategies**
  - **Building Relationships**: Foster positive relationships with your tenants by being responsive to their needs and concerns. Promptly addressing maintenance issues and providing excellent service can encourage tenants to stay longer.
  - **Lease Renewals**: Offer lease renewals well in advance of the lease expiration date. Providing incentives for early renewals, such as minor upgrades or rent discounts, can encourage tenants to stay.
  - **Maintaining the Property**: Regularly maintain and improve the property to ensure it remains in excellent condition. A well-

maintained property reduces tenant complaints and increases satisfaction.
- **Minimizing Turnover and Ensuring Occupancy**
    - **Flexible Lease Terms**: Offer flexible lease terms to accommodate different tenant needs. Short-term leases, month-to-month options, or longer leases can attract a wider range of tenants.
    - **Rent Incentives**: Provide rent incentives, such as a free month's rent or reduced security deposit, to attract and retain tenants. Incentives can be particularly effective during slower rental seasons.
    - **Thorough Tenant Screening**: Implement a rigorous tenant screening process to select reliable tenants who are likely to stay longer. Checking credit scores, employment history, and previous rental references can help identify responsible tenants.

By setting competitive rent prices, investing in value-adding renovations, and implementing effective tenant retention strategies, landlords can maximize their rental income and ensure long-term profitability. Reducing vacancy rates and maintaining a high-quality property will attract reliable tenants and contribute to a steady and increased rental income stream.

6. Case Studies

1. Successful Rental Property Investments
- **Analysis of Profitable Investments**
    - **Examining Case Studies**: Analyze specific examples of rental property investments that yielded significant returns. For instance, a case study might involve an investor who purchased a multi-family property in a burgeoning urban area, renovated it to enhance its appeal, and subsequently raised rental rates. These detailed narratives can illustrate the importance of strategic location selection, property improvement, and effective tenant management.
    - **Identifying Common Strategies**: Successful investors often share common strategies such as thorough market research, prudent financial planning, and proactive property management. For example, they

might employ value-adding renovations to increase rental income or focus on high-demand neighborhoods to ensure steady occupancy.

- **Lessons Learned from Experienced Investors**
    - **Learning from Mistakes**: Experienced investors often face challenges such as unexpected maintenance costs, tenant disputes, or market downturns. Case studies can highlight how these investors overcame such challenges, providing valuable lessons. For instance, one investor might have mitigated risk by diversifying their property portfolio, while another might have implemented stringent tenant screening processes to reduce turnover and late payments.
    - **Adapting to Market Changes**: Successful investors are often those who adapt to changing market conditions. Case studies might show how investors adjusted their strategies in response to economic shifts, such as focusing on affordable housing

during a recession or investing in luxury rentals during a market boom.

2. **Challenges and Solutions**
   - **Common Problems Faced by Landlords**
     - **Tenant Disputes**: Issues such as non-payment of rent, noise complaints, and lease violations are common. Landlords might face legal challenges when trying to evict problematic tenants.
     - **Property Damage**: Damage to the property, whether intentional or accidental, can result in significant repair costs and downtime.
     - **Maintenance Challenges**: Regular maintenance can be time-consuming and costly. Emergencies such as plumbing leaks or electrical failures require prompt attention to prevent further damage and ensure tenant satisfaction.
   - **Strategies for Overcoming Challenges**
     - **Comprehensive Lease Agreements**: Crafting a detailed lease agreement that clearly outlines tenant responsibilities, rent payment terms, and penalties for violations

can prevent disputes. Include clauses that cover property maintenance, noise levels, and eviction procedures.
- **Open Communication with Tenants**: Maintaining open lines of communication helps address issues before they escalate. Regular check-ins and being responsive to tenant concerns can build a positive landlord-tenant relationship.
- **Emergency Fund**: Establishing an emergency fund to cover unexpected expenses ensures that you can handle urgent repairs without financial strain. This proactive measure helps maintain the property's condition and tenant satisfaction.

7. Tax Implications and Legal Considerations

1. Understanding Rental Income Taxes
- **Tax Deductions and Credits**
  - **Mortgage Interest and Property Taxes**: Deducting mortgage interest and property taxes can significantly reduce taxable rental income. These are among the largest and

most common deductions available to rental property owners.

- o **Insurance and Maintenance**: Expenses for property insurance and routine maintenance are deductible. This includes costs for repairs, landscaping, and pest control.
- o **Depreciation**: The IRS allows property owners to depreciate the value of their rental property over a period, typically 27.5 years for residential properties. This non-cash deduction can substantially lower taxable income.
- o **Energy-Efficient Upgrades**: Tax credits may be available for improvements that increase the energy efficiency of rental properties, such as installing solar panels or energy-efficient windows.

- **Filing Rental Income on Tax Returns**
  - o **Accurate Reporting**: It is crucial to accurately report all rental income and related expenses on your tax return. Misreporting can result in penalties and interest.

- **Accounting Software and Professional Help**: Using accounting software can streamline the process of tracking income and expenses. Hiring a tax professional can ensure compliance with tax laws and optimize deductions.

2. Legal Requirements
- **Landlord-Tenant Laws**
    - **Eviction Procedures**: Understanding the legal steps required for evicting a tenant is crucial. This includes providing proper notice, filing necessary court documents, and following through with court-ordered procedures.
    - **Security Deposit Regulations**: Laws governing the collection, handling, and return of security deposits vary by state and locality. Familiarize yourself with these regulations to avoid legal disputes.
    - **Habitability Standards**: Ensure your property meets all habitability standards, including providing safe and functional plumbing, heating, and electrical systems.

Failure to comply can result in legal action from tenants.

- **Compliance with Local Regulations**
    - **Zoning Laws and Building Codes**: Ensure that your property complies with local zoning laws and building codes. This includes obtaining the necessary permits for renovations and repairs.
    - **Health and Safety Regulations**: Adhere to regulations that ensure the property is safe and habitable. This includes regular inspections for issues such as lead paint, asbestos, and mold.
    - **Permits for Renovations**: When making significant renovations, obtain the required permits from local authorities. Unpermitted work can result in fines and legal complications.

By understanding the intricacies of rental property management, tax implications, and legal considerations, landlords can optimize their investment returns and ensure compliance with all relevant laws and regulations.

In conclusion, rental property investing is a dynamic and powerful avenue to building substantial wealth and achieving the coveted goal of financial independence. The journey towards success in this realm involves a deep understanding of the diverse types of rental properties available, from residential to commercial, each presenting its own unique set of opportunities and considerations. By strategically navigating the investment process, from meticulous research and financial planning to leveraging the expertise of seasoned professionals, investors can lay the foundation for a robust and lucrative rental property portfolio.

Effective property management is pivotal to the long-term success of any rental venture. This encompasses not just the practical aspects of maintenance and tenant relations but also the strategic utilization of tools such as screening processes, lease agreements, and property upgrades to optimize rental income and enhance the overall value of the investment. By embracing a proactive and diligent approach to property management, investors can minimize vacancies, mitigate risks, and foster positive relationships with tenants, ultimately contributing to the overall profitability and sustainability of their rental business.

The case studies and insights shared by experienced investors serve as invaluable guides, shedding light on the tangible rewards and inevitable challenges that come with rental property investments. Their stories underscore the importance of financial prudence, continuous learning, and strict adherence to legal and tax obligations. By learning from the successes and pitfalls of others, aspiring investors can forge their own path, armed with knowledge and realistic expectations, thus increasing their chances of long-term prosperity in the rental property arena.

Diversifying income streams through rental properties is not merely a strategic choice but also a gateway to financial security and newfound opportunities. It empowers individuals to reduce their reliance on a single source of income, mitigating risks and providing a buffer against economic fluctuations. Furthermore, the passive income generated from rental properties can open doors to additional investment possibilities, be it expanding one's real estate portfolio or exploring other asset classes. This diversification not only strengthens one's financial foundation but also fosters the potential for exponential growth and wealth accumulation.

Embracing the rental property journey demands a commitment to ongoing education and adaptability. Market dynamics and regulations evolve, requiring investors to stay abreast of industry trends, emerging technologies, and legal updates. By cultivating a network of trusted professionals, including realtors, property managers, and financial advisors, investors can access a wealth of knowledge and expertise to make well-informed decisions.

Additionally, staying engaged with industry associations, attending seminars, and leveraging online resources can further enhance one's understanding of the rental property landscape, ensuring a more prosperous and rewarding investment trajectory.

In closing, the path to financial freedom through rental property investing is within reach for those who are willing to dedicate themselves to the process. It demands a blend of strategic thinking, financial acumen, and a steadfast commitment to excellence in property management. By diligently implementing the insights gained from this course, investors can confidently embark on their rental property journey, armed with the tools necessary to create a stable and profitable income stream, ultimately achieving their financial aspirations and securing a brighter future.

Chapter 6

Dividend Income

1. Definition and Overview

Dividend income represents a fundamental concept in the world of investing, signifying the distribution of profits by a company to its shareholders. This income stream is a way for investors to directly partake in the success and prosperity of the companies they own a stake in. Dividends can be thought of as a reward for investing in and committing to a particular company's journey. They are a tangible demonstration of a company's financial health and maturity, reflecting its ability to generate sufficient profits to share with its investors.

Dividends can be distributed in various forms, each offering distinct advantages and considerations:

Cash Dividends: By far the most common type, cash dividends involve the payment of profits in cold, hard currency. Shareholders receive a specified amount of cash for each share they own. This form of dividend is straightforward and provides immediate liquidity to investors.

Stock Dividends: Instead of cash, companies may opt to

distribute additional shares of their stock as dividends. This approach is often used when a company wants to retain its cash for reinvestment or expansion. Stock dividends have the effect of increasing the total number of shares outstanding, diluting the ownership percentage of existing shareholders but providing them with more units of ownership.

Property Dividends: On rare occasions, companies may distribute physical assets or property to shareholders as dividends. This could include real estate, artwork, or other valuable items. Property dividends are less common and may be subject to unique tax treatments.

Other Forms: Dividends can also take the form of options, warrants, or even shares in a spin-off company. These less traditional forms of dividends offer shareholders alternative ways to benefit from the company's success.

Dividend income stands apart from other forms of investment income, such as interest income or capital gains. Interest income, for instance, is generated from lending activities, such as bonds or savings accounts, and typically provides a fixed rate of return.

Capital gains, on the other hand, result from the sale of an asset, such as stocks or real estate, and represent the profit realized from the appreciation of that asset's value. Dividend income, in contrast, is a direct distribution of a company's profits, providing a more immediate and tangible return on investment.

2. Benefits and Drawbacks: Weighing the Pros and Cons

Investing with a focus on dividend income offers a multitude of advantages to investors, enhancing their financial prospects and providing a measure of stability:

Passive Income: Dividend income offers investors a passive and recurring source of cash flow. This income can be particularly attractive to those seeking financial freedom or looking to supplement their earned income. The beauty of dividend income is that it requires minimal ongoing effort, as the profits are distributed directly by the companies in which investors choose to invest.

Long-Term Growth: Dividend-paying companies often exhibit a strong track record of financial stability and growth. Reinvesting dividends over time can lead to the power of compounding, resulting in substantial wealth accumulation. The discipline of consistently investing and reinvesting dividends has the potential to generate impressive long-term returns.

Indicator of Company Health: Dividend income serves as a barometer of a company's financial health and stability. Companies that pay dividends tend to be more established, profitable, and well-managed. They have the financial wherewithal to share their profits with shareholders, signaling a lower risk of financial distress.

However, it is important to acknowledge the potential challenges and drawbacks of investing for dividend income:

Tax Implications: Dividend income is typically subject to taxation, and the rates can vary depending on the type of dividend and the investor's overall tax bracket. For instance, qualified dividends, which meet certain requirements, may be taxed at lower capital gains rates, while ordinary dividends are taxed as regular income. Investors need to be mindful of the potential tax burden and plan accordingly.

Lower Dividend Yields in Certain Industries: Not all industries are created equal when it comes to dividend yields. Sectors such as technology or high-growth industries may prioritize reinvesting profits into research and development or expansion, resulting in lower dividend payouts. Investors seeking higher yields may need to look beyond these sectors, understanding the trade-off between dividend income and the potential for higher capital appreciation.

Volatility and Market Risk: Dividend-paying stocks, like any equity investment, are subject to market volatility and the potential for capital losses. While dividend income can provide a measure of stability, it does not insulate investors from broader market downturns or industry-specific risks. Diversification becomes crucial to mitigate these risks and protect against potential declines in dividend payouts.

3. Identifying Dividend-Paying Investments

Stocks and Shares: When it comes to earning dividend income, stocks and shares are the most traditional and widely recognized avenue. Investing in dividend-paying stocks provides shareholders with the opportunity to directly benefit from the success and profitability of the companies they own. Dividend-paying companies often have a strong track record of financial stability and a commitment to sharing their profits with investors.

Factors to Consider When Choosing Dividend-Paying Stocks
- Dividend History and Consistency: Look for companies with a long and consistent track record of paying dividends. Consistency is key, as it demonstrates the company's ability to maintain payouts over time, even during economic downturns.

- Dividend Yield: The dividend yield, calculated by dividing the annual dividend amount by the current stock price, provides insight into the income potential of the investment. However, it is important to consider that extremely high yields may signal underlying risks or financial distress.
- Financial Health and Stability: Assess the overall financial health of the company, including its revenue growth, profitability, and debt levels. A company with strong financial fundamentals is more likely to sustain and increase its dividend payouts over time.
- Industry Presence and Competitive Advantage: Consider the company's position within its industry and its competitive advantage. Look for companies with a strong market share, a unique value proposition, or a history of innovation, as these factors can contribute to long-term success and, by extension, sustained dividend payouts.

Examples of Dividend-Paying Stocks
- Johnson & Johnson (JNJ): A stalwart in the healthcare sector, JNJ has a long history of dividend payments, increasing its payouts for over 50 consecutive years. The company's commitment to shareholder returns, coupled with its diverse business segments, makes it a favorite among dividend investors.

- Coca-Cola (KO): KO is renowned for its consistent and growing dividend payouts. With a global presence and a portfolio of well-known brands, Coca-Cola has rewarded shareholders with steadily increasing dividends for decades.
- Procter & Gamble (PG): PG, a consumer goods giant, has a strong track record of dividend payments and increases. The company's focus on innovation and brand strength has resulted in steady financial performance, supporting its dividend policy.

Mutual Funds and ETFs: Diversified Dividend Income

For investors seeking a more diversified approach to dividend income, mutual funds and exchange-traded funds (ETFs) offer an attractive option. These investment vehicles provide exposure to a carefully curated basket of dividend-paying stocks, managed by professional investment managers.

Benefits of Mutual Funds and ETFs

- Diversification: By pooling investor funds to purchase a diverse range of stocks, mutual funds and ETFs reduce the risk associated with individual stock picking. This diversification helps mitigate the impact of any single stock's performance on the overall portfolio.

- Professional Management: The expertise of fund managers, who conduct extensive research and analysis, can be invaluable. These professionals actively monitor the dividend-paying landscape, making informed decisions on stock selection and portfolio construction.
- Higher Yields: Dividend-focused mutual funds and ETFs often target higher-yielding stocks or employ strategies to enhance dividend income. This can result in potentially higher payouts for investors compared to individual stock picking.
- Accessibility: Mutual funds and ETFs offer investors access to a wide array of dividend-paying companies, including those that may be challenging or costly to purchase individually, such as foreign or small-cap stocks.

Examples of Dividend-Focused Mutual Funds and ETFs

- Vanguard Dividend Appreciation Index Fund (VIG): This ETF tracks an index of companies with a history of increasing dividend payments. With a low expense ratio, VIG provides exposure to a diversified portfolio of large-cap dividend growers.
- Schwab U.S. Dividend Equity Fund (SCHD): SCHD is a mutual fund that focuses on high-dividend-yielding stocks with strong fundamentals. The fund's

management team employs a rigorous selection process, resulting in a portfolio of quality dividend payers.
- iShares Core High Dividend ETF (HDV): HDV seeks to track an index of companies with relatively high dividend yields. By targeting specific sectors and employing a screening process, this ETF aims to provide investors with a steady stream of dividend income.

4. Real Estate Investment Trusts (REITs)

Real Estate Investment Trusts (REITs) offer a unique and compelling opportunity to invest in dividend income derived from the real estate sector. REITs are companies that own, operate, or finance income-producing real estate, providing investors with the benefits of real estate ownership without the challenges of direct property management.

How REITs Work
- Portfolio of Properties: REITs own and manage a diverse portfolio of income-generating real estate assets, which may include office buildings, retail spaces, apartments, warehouses, or other property types.
- Passive Income through Rent Collection: REITs generate revenue primarily through the collection of rent from tenants leasing their properties. This rental income

provides a steady cash flow, similar to the way dividend-paying companies distribute profits.
- Legal Requirements and Tax Advantages: To qualify as a REIT, certain legal requirements must be met, including distributing at least 90% of taxable income to shareholders as dividends. In return, REITs enjoy favorable tax treatment, avoiding corporate income taxes at the entity level.

Benefits and Risks for Investors
- High Dividend Yields: REITs are known for their attractive dividend payouts, often yielding higher than the average stock. This makes them a favored choice for income-oriented investors.
- Diversification and Lower Correlation: Investing in REITs provides portfolio diversification, as real estate tends to have a lower correlation with traditional stocks and bonds. This helps reduce overall portfolio risk.
- Long-term Capital Appreciation: In addition to dividend income, REITs offer the potential for capital appreciation over time, driven by increases in property values and rental rates.
- Professional Management: Similar to mutual funds, REITs are managed by real estate experts who handle the complexities of property acquisition, management, and tenant relations.

However, it is important to consider the potential risks associated with REITs, including the impact of rising interest rates, high management fees, and the inherent volatility of the real estate market. Due diligence and a comprehensive understanding of the REIT structure are crucial before investing.

5. Strategies for Maximizing Dividend Income: Unlocking the Full Potential

a. Long-Term Investing: Harnessing the Power of Compound Interest

One of the most effective strategies for maximizing dividend income is embracing a long-term investment horizon. The concept of compound interest, where dividends are reinvested over time, can lead to exponential growth in an investor's portfolio. By opting for dividend reinvestment, investors harness the power of time and compounding to their advantage.

Understanding Compound Interest

Compound interest is the process by which dividends are reinvested to generate earnings, and those earnings, in turn, generate their own earnings. Over time, this recursive cycle results in accelerated wealth accumulation. The magic of compound interest lies in the fact that not only does the initial investment grow, but the reinvested dividends also generate returns, creating a snowball effect.

Illustrating the Power of Compound Interest

Let's illustrate the impact of compound interest with an example. Assume an investor purchases $10,000 worth of a dividend-paying stock, with an initial dividend yield of 4%. In the first year, the investor receives $400 in dividend income. If the investor chooses to reinvest these dividends, the $400 is used to purchase additional shares of the stock. In the second year, the investor earns dividends on the larger number of shares, resulting in a higher dividend income. This cycle continues, with the reinvested dividends generating their own returns.

Here's a simplified calculation to demonstrate the potential wealth accumulation over a 20-year period:

Year 1: Initial investment of $10,000 with a 4% dividend yield earns $400 in dividends.

Year 2: Reinvesting the $400 dividends results in a larger number of shares and a total dividend income of $416 (assuming a constant dividend yield).

Year 5: Through compound interest, the dividend income grows to $519.

Year 10: The dividend income has increased to $739.

Year 20: After two decades of compound interest, the dividend income reaches an impressive $1,897.

This example underscores the transformative power of compound interest. By reinvesting dividends, the initial investment of $10,000 generates nearly $2,000 in annual dividend income after 20 years, representing a substantial return on the original capital outlay.

b. Dividend Growth Investing

Dividend growth investing is a strategy that focuses on selecting companies with a track record of consistently increasing their dividend payouts over time. This approach blends elements of both growth and value investing, offering investors the potential for higher yields and capital appreciation.

Understanding Dividend Growth Investing

Dividend growth investing hinges on the premise that a company's ability to consistently increase its dividend payouts is indicative of strong financial health and profitability. These companies often exhibit a commitment to returning value to shareholders while also reinvesting in their business for future growth.

Benefits of Dividend Growth Investing

- Higher Yields Over Time: By investing in companies that regularly increase their dividends, investors can benefit from higher yields as their holdings mature. The

combination of dividend growth and compounding can lead to substantial income potential.
- Blend of Growth and Value: Dividend growth investing strikes a balance between growth and value. It offers the stability and income of value investing, coupled with the potential for capital appreciation associated with growth stocks.
- Inflation Protection: Dividend growth investing provides a measure of protection against inflation. As companies increase their dividend payouts over time, investors' purchasing power is preserved, ensuring that their income keeps pace with rising prices.

Examples of Dividend Growth Investing in Action
- Dividend Aristocrats: A well-known group of companies known as Dividend Aristocrats have a track record of increasing their dividends for at least 25 consecutive years. These companies, spanning various sectors, include household names like Walmart, Coca-Cola, and Procter & Gamble. Investing in Dividend Aristocrats provides a strong foundation for dividend growth portfolios.
- Sector Rotation Strategies: Dividend growth investors may also employ sector rotation strategies, allocating a larger portion of their portfolio to sectors with higher dividend growth potential. For example, focusing on

technology or healthcare sectors, which tend to exhibit higher dividend growth rates, can boost overall portfolio yields.

c. High-Yield Strategies

High-yield dividend stocks offer investors the allure of substantial income potential. However, it is crucial to approach these investments with caution, as extremely high yields may signal underlying financial distress or unsustainable payout ratios.

Understanding High-Yield Dividend Stocks

High-yield dividend stocks are those that offer dividend payouts significantly higher than the market average. These stocks often attract income-focused investors seeking immediate returns. However, it is essential to distinguish between healthy high-yield stocks and those that may pose risks.

Benefits and Risks of High-Yield Strategies

- Higher Income Potential: High-yield dividend stocks provide investors with the opportunity to generate substantial income, often exceeding the returns offered by more conservative dividend payers.
- Risk of Financial Distress: It is important to recognize that extremely high dividend yields may indicate financial challenges within a company. A company may

be struggling to maintain its operations or facing declining profitability, leading to unsustainable dividend payouts.
- Volatility and Capital Risk: High-yield stocks can be more volatile, exhibiting larger price swings than the broader market. Investors not only face the risk of lower dividend payouts but also the potential for capital losses if the stock price declines.

Due Diligence and Risk Mitigation

To navigate the risks associated with high-yield dividend stocks, investors must conduct thorough due diligence:
- Financial Health Assessment: Scrutinize the company's financial statements, looking for stable revenue growth, healthy profit margins, and manageable debt levels. Ensure that the dividend payout ratio is sustainable and that the company has sufficient cash flow to support dividend payments.
- Industry and Sector Analysis: Consider the broader industry dynamics and the potential impact on dividend sustainability. Some sectors, such as utilities or consumer staples, are known for their stable and predictable dividend payouts, while others may be more susceptible to economic cycles.
- Peer Comparison: Compare the dividend yield and payout ratio of the stock in question to those of its peers

within the same industry. This can help identify outliers that may warrant further investigation.

6. Evaluating Company Health and Sustainability

a. Financial Analysis: When considering an investment in dividend-paying stocks, it is imperative to assess the financial health of the underlying company. This evaluation ensures that the company has the stability and profitability necessary to support stable and consistent dividend payouts over time.

Key Financial Ratios for Dividend Investors

- Dividend Payout Ratio: The dividend payout ratio is calculated by dividing the total dividends paid by the company's net income. This ratio indicates the proportion of earnings that are distributed to shareholders as dividends. A consistently high payout ratio may suggest a risk of future dividend cuts, especially if the company experiences earnings volatility. Ideally, investors should look for companies with a sustainable and consistent payout ratio, typically in the range of 50-70%.
- Dividend Coverage Ratio: Also known as the dividend coverage metric, this ratio is calculated by dividing the company's net income or free cash flow by the total dividends paid. It assesses the company's ability to cover

its dividend payments from its profits. A coverage ratio above 1 indicates that the company is generating sufficient earnings to support its dividend policy.

- Return on Equity (ROE): ROE measures the company's profitability relative to shareholder equity. It is calculated by dividing the company's net income by its shareholders' equity. A high ROE indicates that the company is efficiently utilizing its equity to generate profits, which can support dividend payouts and future growth.

- Debt-to-Equity Ratio: Analyzing a company's debt levels is crucial, as excessive debt may hinder its ability to sustain dividend payments. The debt-to-equity ratio compares a company's total liabilities to shareholders' equity. A high debt burden may indicate financial risk and potential challenges in maintaining dividend payouts, especially if interest rates rise.

- Free Cash Flow (FCF): FCF represents the cash flow available to a company after accounting for operating expenses and capital expenditures. Positive and growing FCF indicates that the company has the financial flexibility to support dividend payments, invest in growth opportunities, or repurchase shares.

Interpreting Financial Statements

Beyond financial ratios, investors should also review the

company's financial statements, including the income statement, balance sheet, and cash flow statement. These statements provide insights into revenue growth trends, profitability margins, cash generation capabilities, and potential red flags, such as increasing debt levels or declining profitability.

Industry and Market Considerations

Evaluating the stability and prospects of the industry in which a company operates is crucial for assessing dividend sustainability. External factors, such as industry trends, competitive landscapes, and economic cycles, can significantly influence a company's ability to maintain and grow its dividend payouts.

b. Industry Trends and Dynamics

Consider the maturity and growth prospects of the industry. Industries with stable and predictable cash flows, such as consumer staples or utilities, often provide a more reliable foundation for dividend payments. In contrast, industries experiencing rapid technological changes or regulatory shifts may pose higher risks to dividend sustainability.

Competitive Landscape

Assess the company's competitive position within its industry. A company with a strong market share, unique competitive advantages, or brand recognition is more likely to sustain its profitability and, by extension, its dividend payouts. Conversely, a company facing intense competition or market disruption may struggle to maintain dividend growth.

Economic Cycles and Market Conditions
Dividend sustainability can be influenced by broader economic cycles and market conditions. During economic downturns or recessions, companies may experience declining revenues and profitability, which could impact their ability to maintain dividend payments. Conversely, companies operating in industries that are less sensitive to economic cycles may provide more stable dividend streams.

c. Management and Corporate Governance
The quality of a company's management team and its corporate governance practices play a pivotal role in dividend sustainability. Effective management ensures prudent financial decision-making, strategic allocation of resources, and alignment with shareholder interests.

Transparent Financial Reporting
Investors should seek companies that provide clear, transparent, and timely financial reporting. Accurate and comprehensive financial disclosures enable investors to assess the company's financial health and make informed decisions. Red flags include complex or opaque financial statements, inconsistent reporting practices, or a lack of disclosure regarding dividend policies.

Executive Compensation Structures

Examine the compensation structures of the company's executive team. Ideally, executive compensation should be aligned with the interests of shareholders, including dividend stability and long-term growth. Avoid companies where executive compensation appears excessive or disconnected from the company's financial performance.

Shareholder Alignment and Corporate Governance Practices

Assess the company's track record of shareholder returns, including dividend payments and share repurchase programs. Look for companies that prioritize shareholder value and maintain good corporate governance practices, such as independent board members, ethical business conduct, and shareholder voting rights.

7. Case Studies

To illustrate the importance of management and corporate governance, consider the following examples:

Case Study 1: A company with a strong track record of dividend growth is led by a management team known for its transparency and shareholder focus. The CEO's compensation is largely tied to the company's financial performance and dividend stability, creating a strong alignment of interests with investors.

Case Study 2: In contrast, a company in a regulated industry faces scrutiny over its executive compensation structure. The management team has been criticized for excessive bonuses and a lack of transparency in financial reporting. This raises concerns about the alignment of interests between management and shareholders.

8. A Step-by-Step Guide to Starting Dividend Investing

a. Setting Investment Goals

The first step in embarking on dividend investing is to define your investment goals and risk tolerance. This foundational step ensures that your dividend strategy aligns with your broader financial objectives and personal circumstances.

- Determining Investment Objectives: Ask yourself: What are your primary goals for investing in dividend-paying stocks? Are you seeking current income, long-term capital appreciation, or a combination of both? Defining your objectives will guide your stock selection, sector allocation, and overall portfolio construction.
- Assessing Risk Tolerance: Risk tolerance refers to the degree of volatility and potential loss you are comfortable with in pursuit of your investment goals. It is influenced by factors such as your age, income, financial obligations, and overall investment horizon. A

younger investor may have a higher risk tolerance, allowing for a more aggressive dividend strategy, while a retiree may prioritize capital preservation and opt for a more conservative approach.

b. Research and Due Diligence

Conducting thorough research and due diligence is essential before investing in dividend-paying stocks. This process involves analyzing financial metrics, conducting industry research, and considering company-specific factors to make well-informed investment decisions.

Financial Metrics and Ratios

- Dividend Payout Ratio: Assess the company's dividend payout ratio to ensure it is sustainable and in line with industry peers. A consistently high payout ratio may indicate a risk of future dividend cuts.
- Dividend Growth Rate: Look for companies with a history of consistently increasing their dividend payouts. Steady dividend growth indicates financial health and a commitment to returning value to shareholders.
- Dividend Yield: Evaluate the dividend yield relative to the stock's price. While a high yield may be attractive, it should be considered alongside other financial metrics to ensure sustainability.

- Earnings per Share (EPS): EPS reflects the company's profitability on a per-share basis. A rising EPS trend is generally positive for dividend sustainability.
- Return on Equity (ROE): ROE measures how effectively the company utilizes shareholders' equity to generate profits. A high and improving ROE indicates efficient capital allocation.

Industry Research and Competitive Analysis
- Industry Dynamics: Understand the industry in which the company operates, including its growth prospects, regulatory environment, and competitive landscape. Assess the stability and maturity of the industry, as this can impact dividend sustainability.
- Competitive Advantage: Evaluate the company's competitive position within its industry. Look for unique capabilities, brand recognition, or technological advantages that can contribute to long-term success and dividend growth.
- Market Share and Customer Loyalty: Consider the company's market share and the loyalty of its customer base. Strong market positioning can provide a buffer during economic downturns and support dividend stability.

Company-Specific Considerations
- Business Model and Revenue Streams: Assess the company's business model and the stability of its revenue streams. Diversified revenue sources can enhance dividend sustainability.
- Management Track Record: Evaluate the management team's experience, expertise, and track record of shareholder value creation. Transparent and ethical management practices are positive indicators.
- News and Analyst Reports: Stay informed about company-specific news, earnings reports, and analyst recommendations. These sources can provide insights into the company's financial health and future prospects.

c. Building a Portfolio

Constructing a diversified dividend portfolio involves selecting a range of dividend-paying stocks across sectors and industries, allocating capital based on your investment goals and risk tolerance.

Stock Selection
- Dividend Aristocrats and Dividend Kings: Consider investing in Dividend Aristocrats (companies with 25+ years of consecutive dividend increases) or Dividend Kings (50+ years). These companies have a proven track record of dividend stability and growth.

- Sector Allocation: Diversify your portfolio across sectors to reduce risk. Include a mix of defensive sectors, such as consumer staples and utilities, along with growth-oriented sectors like technology and healthcare.
- Stock Screening and Fundamental Analysis: Utilize stock screening tools to identify potential dividend-paying stocks based on your criteria. Conduct fundamental analysis to assess financial health, growth prospects, and dividend sustainability.

Portfolio Construction
- Core Holdings: Establish a core group of stable, blue-chip dividend payers as the foundation of your portfolio. These companies should have a long history of dividend payments and solid financial footing.
- Satellite Holdings: Supplement your core holdings with satellite positions in companies offering higher dividend yields or growth potential. These may involve more risk but can enhance overall portfolio returns.
- Regular Review and Rebalancing: Periodically review your portfolio to ensure it aligns with your investment goals and risk tolerance. Rebalance as needed to maintain your desired sector allocation and risk profile.

d. Tax Considerations

Dividend income is generally subject to taxation, and it's

important to understand the tax implications to maximize your after-tax returns.

Tax Rates and Withholding Taxes
- Qualified Dividends: In many countries, dividends that meet certain requirements, such as holding periods and company residency, may qualify for lower tax rates similar to long-term capital gains.
- Ordinary Dividends: Dividends that do not meet the criteria for qualified dividends are typically taxed as ordinary income, which may result in higher tax rates.
- Withholding Taxes: Dividends from foreign companies may be subject to withholding taxes, reducing the amount you receive. Understand the tax treaties and withholding rates applicable to your investments.

Tax-Advantaged Accounts
- Retirement Plans: Holding dividend-paying stocks in tax-advantaged accounts, such as IRAs or 401(k)s, can provide tax benefits. Dividends earned in these accounts may be tax-deferred or tax-free, enhancing your overall returns.
- Tax-Efficient Portfolio Management: Consider tax implications when constructing your portfolio. For example, hold high-yield dividend stocks in tax-

advantaged accounts to minimize the impact of ordinary income tax rates.

Conclusion: Taking the First Steps with Confidence

By following these steps—setting investment goals, conducting thorough research, building a diversified portfolio, and understanding tax considerations—you'll be well on your way to becoming a savvy dividend investor. Remember that dividend investing is a long-term strategy, and it requires patience and discipline. Stay informed about market trends, company developments, and economic factors that may impact your holdings. Regularly review and adjust your portfolio as necessary to align with your investment plan.

In conclusion, building a robust dividend portfolio involves a thoughtful and methodical approach. By setting clear investment goals, conducting diligent research, and constructing a diversified portfolio, you can position yourself to achieve your financial objectives. Remember that dividend investing is a journey, and staying committed to your strategy, even during market fluctuations, will enhance your chances of success.

Chapter 7
Royalties

1. Introduction to Royalties

I'd like to delve into the fascinating world of royalties and uncover the intriguing history behind this concept. You see, royalties are not merely about monetary transactions; they represent the value we place on intellectual property and natural resources. So, picture this as a journey through time, where we'll explore the evolution of royalties and their significance in our modern world.

Once upon a time, in the grand halls of monarchs and kingdoms, the concept of royalties first emerged. Imagine a king, sitting upon his throne, granting privileges and land to his loyal subjects. In return, these subjects would provide regular payments, almost like a tribute, to the monarch. This, my students, was one of the earliest forms of royalties.

Now, fast forward with me to the realm of literature and the arts. Think of the great writers and musicians of the past, like Shakespeare and Beethoven. They, too, relied on royalties for their livelihood. When their works were performed or reproduced, they received payments, ensuring they were compensated for their creative endeavors. This concept of royalties helped foster artistic innovation and protected the rights of these visionary creators.

But royalties are not limited to the creative arts. In the realm of science and invention, patents come into play. Imagine a brilliant inventor, toiling day and night to create a groundbreaking machine or process. Through the system of royalties, this inventor can be assured that their intellectual property is protected, and they receive compensation each time their invention is utilized.

And let's not forget the treasures hidden within our planet. Natural resources, such as minerals, oil, and gas, also fall under the umbrella of royalties. When companies extract these resources from the earth, they pay royalties to the landowners or governments, acknowledging the value of these finite gifts from nature.

So, my dear, royalties are not just about money changing hands. They represent the value we place on ideas, creativity, innovation, and the very resources that sustain our world. The concept of royalties has evolved over centuries, shaping industries and protecting the rights of individuals and organizations alike. And who knows, perhaps one day, you too will be receiving royalties for your own brilliant creations!

2. Types of Royalties: An Exploration

Royalties come in different forms, each tied to specific assets or rights. These financial arrangements serve as the lifeblood for many creators, landowners, and business operators. To understand royalties better, we need to delve into the various forms they take, each connected to distinct assets or rights. This understanding is crucial for anyone looking to identify potential sources of royalty income. Let us explore the three main types: Intellectual Property Royalties, Natural Resource Royalties, and Franchise Royalties.

a. Intellectual Property Royalties: The Creative Revenue Stream

Imagine a talented author, Emily, who has just published her debut novel. As her book hits the shelves, she begins to receive payments known as royalties for each copy sold. These are Intellectual Property Royalties, the fruits of her creative labor. Such royalties aren't limited to books alone. Musicians like John, who writes soul-stirring songs, earn royalties every time their compositions are streamed or purchased. Filmmakers and inventors also benefit similarly, receiving payments whenever their works are utilized. For instance, an inventor like Thomas, who has patented a revolutionary technology, receives royalties from companies that manufacture products using his invention. Intellectual Property Royalties thus serve as a vital income stream for those whose creativity and innovation enrich our lives.

b. Natural Resource Royalties: Profits from the Earth's Bounty

Picture a vast expanse of land owned by the Carter family, rich with oil reserves beneath its surface. When an energy company approaches them to extract this oil, the Carters agree to the extraction but on the condition of receiving regular payments. These payments are Natural Resource Royalties. Companies extracting resources like oil, gas, or minerals from land must compensate the landowners or the government for the right to do so. The amount is typically based on the volume or value of the resources extracted. For instance, as the oil is pumped out and sold, the Carter family receives a percentage of the sales, ensuring they benefit from the natural wealth of their land. Natural Resource Royalties are thus a critical mechanism for sharing the profits derived from exploiting the earth's bounty.

c. Franchise Royalties: The Price of Proven Success

Consider Sarah, an entrepreneur eager to start her own business but wary of the risks involved in building a brand from scratch. She decides to open a franchise of a well-known fast food chain. In return for using the chain's brand, products, and operational systems, Sarah pays Franchise Royalties to the franchisor. This arrangement is common in industries like fast food, retail, and hospitality. Franchise Royalties are typically a percentage of the franchisee's sales, reflecting the value of operating under an established and trusted brand. For Sarah, these royalties are a worthwhile investment, providing her with a proven business model and continuous support, significantly increasing her chances of success. Franchise Royalties, therefore, facilitate the expansion of successful business models while generating revenue for the original brand creators.

3. How Royalties Work

Royalties are typically governed by licensing agreements, which outline the terms of use, payment structures, and other relevant details. These agreements can vary significantly depending on the type of royalty and the parties involved.

Certainly, let's delve into the intricacies of how royalties function, as they play a pivotal role in various industries, particularly in safeguarding the interests of intellectual property owners and ensuring they receive their rightful compensation.

Licensing Agreements

The cornerstone of the royalty system is licensing agreements. These are legally binding contracts between the owner of the intellectual property (the licensor) and the party seeking to use that property (the licensee). Licensing agreements delineate the specific rights and privileges granted to the licensee, setting clear boundaries on how they can utilize the intellectual property. For instance, in the music industry, a licensing agreement might grant a record label the right to reproduce and distribute a musician's songs, with stipulations on the number of copies and the territories where the distribution is allowed.

Equally important in these agreements is the specification of the duration of the license. This could be for a fixed term, like a few years, or it could be ongoing, with provisions for renewal or termination. The duration often depends on the nature of the intellectual property and the intended use.

Payment Structures

The financial aspect of royalties is articulated in the payment structure outlined in the licensing agreement. There are two primary models for royalty payments:

Fixed Amount: In this model, a predetermined sum is set as the royalty for each unit of the intellectual property sold or used. For example, an author might receive $1 as a royalty for every copy of their book sold. This structure is straightforward and easy to calculate.

Percentage of Revenue: Here, the royalty is calculated as a proportion of the revenue generated from the sale of the intellectual property. Using the author example again, they might receive 10% of the sales price of each book sold. This model is often used when the sales price can vary, such as with different book formats (hardcover, paperback, ebook) or in situations where the licensee wants to share the risks and rewards more equally.

The choice between a fixed amount and a percentage depends on various factors, including industry standards, the negotiating power of the parties involved, and the level of risk and reward each party is willing to assume.

Royalty Audits and Compliance

To ensure fairness and accuracy in royalty payments, regular royalty audits are conducted. These audits verify that the licensee is reporting sales or usage accurately and is remitting royalties in accordance with the terms of the licensing agreement. Royalty audits are particularly important when dealing with complex payment structures or when the licensee operates in a less transparent manner.

Compliance with the terms of the licensing agreement is critical. Non-compliance can lead to legal disputes and financial penalties. For instance, if a licensee underreports sales or fails to pay royalties on time, the licensor can take legal action to recoup lost revenue and may even terminate the agreement. Therefore, both parties have a vested interest in ensuring compliance with the agreed-upon terms.

4. Generating Royalties from Intellectual Property

One of the most common ways to earn royalties is through intellectual property. Let's take a comprehensive look at how royalties are generated from various forms of intellectual property, as this is a crucial aspect of monetizing creative works and innovations.

Writing and Publishing Books

Authors have long relied on royalties as a primary source of income from their literary works. The traditional model involves a publishing house acquiring the rights to publish and distribute an author's book. The author then receives a royalty for each copy of the book sold. These royalties are typically calculated as a percentage of the book's sale price, as mentioned earlier. For instance, a standard royalty rate for a hardcover book might be 10-15% of the retail price. So, for a $20 book, the author would earn $2-3 per copy sold.

The advent of self-publishing has also opened new avenues for authors to earn royalties. Through platforms like Amazon Kindle Direct Publishing, authors can retain a higher percentage of the sales revenue, often receiving royalties of up to 70% for ebooks.

This route has empowered many authors to take control of their work's distribution and royalties.

The success of J.K. Rowling, the author of the Harry Potter series, exemplifies the potential for substantial royalty earnings. Not only has she earned royalties from the phenomenal global sales of the books, but the translations and adaptations of her works into movies have also generated significant additional royalty income.

Music Creation and Distribution

In the music industry, royalties are a fundamental way for musicians to monetize their creative output. Musicians earn royalties whenever their music is sold, streamed, or publicly performed. The rise of digital music platforms, such as Spotify, Apple Music, and Amazon Music, has revolutionized how people consume music and, consequently, how musicians earn royalties.

For example, Taylor Swift, a contemporary music icon, has strategically utilized both traditional album sales and streaming platforms to maximize her royalty income. With each album release, she generates substantial revenue from physical and digital sales, and the subsequent streaming of her songs on these platforms generates additional royalties.

The breakdown of music royalties can be complex, with different rates and collection societies involved for mechanical royalties (reproduction and distribution), performance royalties (public performance), and synchronization royalties (use of music in visual media). Nonetheless, the proliferation of streaming services has generally provided musicians with more opportunities to reach audiences and generate royalty income.

Patents and Technological Innovations

Royalties are not limited to creative works; they also play a significant role in the world of innovation and technology. Inventors can license their patented inventions to companies, earning royalties from the sale or use of products incorporating their patented ideas. This provides a financial incentive for inventors to bring their innovations to market without necessarily having to engage in manufacturing and distribution themselves.

A well-known example is George Foreman, a former professional boxer, who licensed his name and likeness for the George Foreman Grill. The grill, featuring a unique fat-reducing design, became a massive commercial success. Foreman earned a royalty on every grill sold, reportedly earning him over $200 million, demonstrating the potential for substantial royalty income from technological innovations.

Apart from earning royalties through intellectual property, one can earn royalties through the following ways:

Natural Resource Royalties

Royalties can be earned from the extraction and utilization of natural resources found on private land. For instance, landowners may receive royalties from mining companies for the right to extract minerals, oil, or natural gas from their property. These royalties are typically based on a percentage of the value or volume of the resources extracted. This system provides an incentive for landowners to permit the responsible development of natural resources, fostering economic growth while ensuring the landowner benefits financially.

Franchising

Franchising is a business model where a franchisee pays a franchise fee to a franchisor in exchange for the right to use their trademarks, trade secrets, and business model. The franchise fee often includes ongoing royalties, which are typically calculated as a percentage of the franchisee's sales revenue. This royalty structure incentivizes the franchisor to provide ongoing support and brand development, as their success is tied to the performance of the franchisees. Examples of industries where franchising is prevalent include fast food (e.g., McDonald's), hospitality (e.g., Marriott), and retail (e.g., 7-Eleven).

Trademark Licensing

Trademark owners can license their trademarks to third parties, allowing them to use the trademark in exchange for royalties. This arrangement is common when a brand wants to expand into new product categories or markets without directly developing and manufacturing the products themselves. For instance, a fashion designer might license their trademark to a fragrance company, earning royalties from the sale of perfumes bearing their name. Effective trademark licensing can enhance brand recognition and generate significant royalty income.

Image and Likeness Rights

Individuals, particularly celebrities and public figures, can monetize their image, likeness, and personality rights. This can involve licensing their name, signature, or likeness for use in advertising, product endorsements, or merchandise. For example, a sports star might license their signature move for use in a video game or their likeness for a line of action figures, earning royalties from the sales of these products. Protecting and leveraging image and likeness rights can be a lucrative source of royalty income for individuals with a strong personal brand.

Royalty Streams in Contracts

Royalties can also be embedded in contractual agreements, where one party agrees to pay royalties to another party as part of a business transaction. For instance, in the film industry, actors, directors, and producers may negotiate for a percentage of a film's profits in addition to their upfront fees. Similarly, in the tech industry, software developers might receive royalties based on the sales of a software product they helped create. These contractual royalty streams provide an ongoing financial stake in the success of a project or venture.

Affiliate Programs

Affiliate programs offer individuals or businesses, known as affiliates, the opportunity to earn royalties or commissions by promoting and selling other people's or companies' products or services. Here's how it typically works:

Affiliation: An affiliate signs up with a company's affiliate program, which could be a retailer, a service provider, or a digital product creator, among others. The affiliate is then provided with unique tracking links or codes that are associated with their account.

Promotion: The affiliate promotes the products or services using their marketing channels, which could include a website, social media, email marketing, or even offline channels like word-of-mouth referrals. The key is to reach an audience interested in the promoted products or services.

Sales and Tracking: When a potential customer clicks on the affiliate's tracking link or uses their code, their activity is recorded by the affiliate program software. If the customer makes a purchase, the sale is attributed to the affiliate, and they earn a commission or royalty for facilitating that sale.

Commission Structure: Commissions can be structured in various ways, such as a percentage of the sale amount, a fixed fee per sale, or even recurring payments for subscription-based products or services. The specific terms and conditions, including the commission rate and payment schedule, are usually outlined in the affiliate program agreement.

5. Legal Aspects of Royalties

Understanding the legal framework surrounding royalties is crucial for protecting one's rights and ensuring fair compensation. The legal aspects can be categorized into several areas, each addressing different types of intellectual property and their respective protections:

Copyright Laws

Copyright laws are designed to protect creative works such as books, music, films, software, and artistic creations. These laws grant creators exclusive rights over their works, allowing them to control how their works are used and distributed. Key points include:

- **Exclusive Rights:** Creators have the exclusive right to reproduce, distribute, perform, display, and create derivative works based on their original creations.
- **Duration:** Copyright protection typically lasts for the life of the author plus an additional 70 years, though this can vary by jurisdiction.
- **Infringement and Enforcement:** Copyright holders can take legal action against unauthorized use or infringement of their works, ensuring they receive appropriate compensation and recognition.

Trademark Considerations

Trademarks protect brand names, logos, slogans, and other identifiers that distinguish goods or services in the marketplace. This protection ensures that only the trademark owner can use these marks in commerce, preventing consumer confusion and protecting brand integrity. Key aspects include:

- **Registration:** While common law rights can arise from the use of a mark in commerce, registering a trademark provides stronger legal protection and nationwide recognition.
- **Exclusive Use:** Trademark owners have the exclusive right to use their marks in connection with the goods or services for which the mark is registered.

- **Renewal:** Trademarks can be renewed indefinitely as long as they are in use, providing ongoing protection for brand identity.
- **Enforcement:** Trademark owners can enforce their rights through litigation, preventing unauthorized use that could dilute or harm their brand.

Patent Laws

Patent laws protect inventions and provide inventors with exclusive rights to make, use, and sell their inventions for a specified period, typically 20 years from the filing date of the patent application. This legal protection encourages innovation by offering inventors a financial incentive and a temporary monopoly on their inventions. Key points include:

- **Types of Patents:** There are different types of patents, including utility patents (for new and useful inventions), design patents (for new and original ornamental designs), and plant patents (for new and distinct plant varieties).
- **Patent Application:** To obtain a patent, an inventor must file a detailed application with the relevant patent office, demonstrating that the invention is novel, non-obvious, and useful.
- **Exclusive Rights:** Patent holders have the exclusive right to prevent others from making, using, selling, or importing the patented invention without permission.

- **Licensing and Royalties:** Patent holders can license their patents to others in exchange for royalty payments, providing a source of ongoing income while allowing others to utilize the invention.

Understanding these legal aspects is essential for anyone involved in creating, using, or commercializing intellectual property. Proper legal protection ensures that creators and inventors are fairly compensated for their work and can continue to innovate and contribute to their respective fields.

6. Strategies to Maximize Royalty Income

Strategy is paramount when aiming to maximize royalty income, and a proactive approach is essential. Here are some key tactics to employ:

Negotiate royalty rates: Royalty rates are often negotiable, and possessing strong negotiation skills can significantly impact your financial gains. Before entering any discussions, ensure you understand the market value of your work and be prepared to justify the worth of your intellectual property. Consider factors such as the uniqueness of your creation, its potential for commercial success, and any relevant industry trends. Being able to articulate the value you bring to the table will strengthen your position during negotiations.

Expand the market reach: Increasing the visibility and accessibility of your work is crucial for boosting royalty income. Explore opportunities to translate your content into different languages, targeting a global audience. International sales can open up new revenue streams and increase your overall earnings. Additionally, leverage digital distribution platforms to maximize your online presence. These platforms often have broad user bases and can help you reach a wider audience with minimal additional effort.

Diversify royalty income streams: Multiple royalty income streams provide financial stability and reduce reliance on a single source of income. For instance, an author can explore opportunities beyond book sales. They might consider licensing their work for movie adaptations or developing merchandise based on their characters or brand. Diversification ensures that you are not solely dependent on one avenue of income, mitigating the potential negative impact of fluctuations in that particular market.

Build and maintain relationships: Nurturing relationships with key stakeholders in the industry can be beneficial. Publishers, producers, and distributors play a crucial role in the success of your work and can influence royalty rates and income. Maintain open lines of communication, attend industry events, and stay connected with individuals who can advocate for your work.

Building a solid network can lead to more opportunities and potentially more favorable terms.

Regularly review and analyze contracts: It is essential to thoroughly understand the terms and conditions of any contract related to your royalty income. Review contracts periodically to ensure you are receiving the agreed-upon royalties and identify any areas where negotiation or renegotiation may be beneficial. Stay informed about industry standards and consult with legal professionals specializing in intellectual property to ensure your interests are protected.

Explore alternative distribution channels: In addition to traditional publishing or distribution methods, consider alternative channels that may offer higher royalty rates or target niche audiences. Self-publishing platforms, for example, often provide authors with greater control over pricing and royalty rates. Exploring these options can help you maximize your income and reach specific markets.

Leverage data and analytics: Utilize data analytics tools provided by distribution platforms or conduct market research to understand better your audience and their preferences. This information can help you make informed decisions about pricing, marketing strategies, and future creations. By aligning your work with market demands, you can increase the potential for higher royalty income.

Protect your intellectual property: Ensure that your intellectual property rights are protected through appropriate copyright, trademark, or patent registrations. This provides legal recourse in the event of unauthorized use or infringement, helping you maintain control over your work and its associated royalties. Stay vigilant in monitoring for any misuse and be prepared to take necessary legal actions.

Stay adaptable and responsive: The market dynamics and consumer preferences can change rapidly, so it is important to stay adaptable. Be responsive to industry trends and be prepared to adjust your strategies accordingly. Continuously seek opportunities to evolve your work and stay relevant in a changing marketplace.

Consider bundling or packaging: In some cases, bundling your work or creating package deals can increase sales and, subsequently, royalty income. For example, offering a discounted price for purchasing multiple books in a series or providing additional content or merchandise with specific purchases can attract buyers and increase revenue.

7. Challenges and Risks

While royalties can be a lucrative source of income, they also come with challenges and risks that need to be carefully managed. Understanding and addressing these challenges is essential for maximizing royalty income and protecting intellectual property.

Piracy and Intellectual Property Theft

Unauthorized use of intellectual property, commonly known as piracy, is a significant threat to creators and rights holders. This can include the illegal distribution of digital media, unauthorized reproductions of works, and counterfeiting. Key points to consider:

- **Impact on Income:** Piracy can lead to substantial financial losses by diverting potential sales and reducing legitimate royalty payments.
- **Legal Protection:** Utilizing legal tools such as copyrights, trademarks, and patents is essential for protecting your work. Registering your intellectual property can strengthen your legal position in case of infringement.
- **Monitoring and Enforcement:** Proactively monitoring for unauthorized use and taking prompt legal action against infringers is crucial. This may involve employing digital rights management (DRM) technologies,

conducting online searches, and working with legal professionals to enforce your rights.

Fluctuations in Market Demand

One of the most significant challenges in earning royalties is the inherent volatility in market demand. The popularity of creative works, whether they are books, music, films, or other forms of intellectual property, can be unpredictable. Several factors contribute to these fluctuations:

- **Changing Consumer Preferences**: Trends in entertainment, technology, and culture can shift rapidly, rendering once-popular works obsolete. For example, a music genre that is highly popular today might fall out of favor tomorrow.
- **Economic Conditions**: Economic downturns can lead to reduced consumer spending on non-essential items like entertainment, affecting sales and, consequently, royalty income.
- **Competition**: The release of new, competing works can impact the demand for existing ones. Staying relevant requires continuous innovation and adaptation to the evolving tastes of the audience.

To mitigate these risks, creators and rights holders must stay attuned to market trends, invest in marketing efforts, and potentially diversify their portfolios. Engaging with audiences through social media and other platforms can also provide valuable insights into changing preferences and help maintain relevance.

Managing and Tracking Royalty Payments

Another significant challenge in the realm of royalties is the management and tracking of payments. As creative works are distributed across multiple platforms and regions, the process of calculating and collecting royalties becomes increasingly complex. The following factors contribute to this complexity:

- **Multiple Revenue Streams**: Royalties can come from various sources such as streaming services, physical sales, licensing deals, and more. Each of these sources may have different payment schedules, rates, and reporting standards.
- **Geographic Discrepancies**: Different countries have varying laws and regulations regarding intellectual property and royalty payments, which can complicate the tracking process.
- **Intermediaries**: Often, royalties pass through multiple intermediaries, such as publishers, agents, or distributors, before reaching the rights holder. Each intermediary may take a commission, and discrepancies can arise at any point in the chain.

To ensure accurate and timely royalty payments, creators and rights holders should implement robust record-keeping practices and conduct regular audits. Leveraging technology such as royalty management software can streamline the process by automating calculations, tracking payments, and generating reports. Additionally, maintaining open communication with intermediaries and legal advisors can help address any issues promptly.

8. Future Trends in Royalties

The world of royalties is a dynamic and ever-changing landscape, shaped by the interplay of technological advancements and market forces. In this article, we will delve into the various factors that are expected to influence the future of royalties, making it an interesting and insightful read for anyone interested in this field.

The Digital Revolution and Its Impact on Royalties

The digital revolution has disrupted virtually every industry, and the world of royalties is no exception. Traditional methods of tracking and earning royalties are being replaced by more efficient and transparent systems, thanks to advances in technology. One of the most promising technologies is blockchain, which has the potential to revolutionize the way royalties are managed. By providing a secure, decentralized, and transparent ledger, blockchain technology can ensure that creators and innovators receive their fair share of royalties, without the need for intermediaries.

Emerging Markets and New Opportunities for Royalties
As emerging markets continue to grow and develop, they offer new opportunities for earning royalties. With increased economic prosperity, these markets are witnessing a surge in demand for creative works and innovations. This creates a fertile ground for creators and innovators to capitalize on, by securing licensing agreements and earning royalties from their intellectual property. By tapping into these emerging markets, creators and innovators can expand their reach and diversify their revenue streams.

Technological Advancements and Their Impact on Royalties
Advances in technology have the potential to create new opportunities for earning royalties. For instance, the rise of artificial intelligence (AI) and machine learning has led to the development of new patentable innovations. As AI continues to evolve, it is likely to give rise to a new wave of technological breakthroughs, which can be protected through patents and licensed to generate royalties.

Furthermore, the increasing use of 3D printing technology has the potential to revolutionize the manufacturing industry, leading to the creation of new products and designs. This can open up new avenues for earning royalties, as creators can license their designs and receive a share of the revenue generated from the sale of these products.

In conclusion, royalties serve as a powerful and sustainable source of wealth for individuals who possess the creativity, innovation, and strategic acumen to leverage their intellectual property. By understanding the diverse types of royalties, their mechanisms, and the strategies to optimize income, individuals can tap into this wealth stream and achieve financial success.

Despite the challenges that may arise, the potential for earning royalties remains significant. As technological advancements continue to drive innovation and creativity, new opportunities for earning royalties will emerge, presenting individuals with the chance to capitalize on their intellectual property and secure their financial future.

To maximize the benefits of royalties as a wealth stream, it is crucial to stay informed about the latest trends and developments in the field. This includes keeping abreast of changes in legislation, technological advancements, and market shifts that may impact the earning potential of royalties. By adapting to these changes and refining their strategies accordingly, individuals can ensure that they remain at the forefront of this dynamic and lucrative industry.

In summary, the world of royalties offers a wealth of opportunities for those who are willing to invest in their creativity and innovation. By understanding the intricacies of this industry and staying informed about the latest trends and developments, individuals can harness the power of royalties to achieve sustainable financial success. With determination, perseverance, and a commitment to excellence, anyone can unlock the potential of royalties and create a prosperous future.

www.ingramcontent.com/pod-product-compliance
Lightning Source LLC
Chambersburg PA
CBHW031620210526
45464CB00004B/1674